American English

Phrasal Verbs
and collocations

Michael Barlow and Stephanie Burdine

ISBN: 978-940753-18-1

Revised 1

Athelstan
2476 Bolsover St, Ste 464
Houston TX 77005
USA

www.athel.com
www.corpuslab.com
info@athel.com

To the Student

The CorpusLAB series of books are based on computer-aided analysis of spoken and written American English. By studying the exercises in this book, you will be learning the most frequent phrasal verbs and associated phrases (collocations) in American English and you will be working with sentences based on real American English.

American Phrasal Verbs is designed to help you improve your understanding of the most frequently used phrasal verbs in everyday English. The phrasal verbs and the phrases and sentences used in this book have been selected on the basis of an analysis of real American English: both spoken and written.

Frequency. Phrasal verbs are very common in English, especially spoken English. The frequency is indicated at the top of each unit by a number of circles.

The top line shows the frequency in speech and the second line shows the frequency in writing. All the phrasal verbs in this book are very frequent in English.

Meaning. We give several common meanings for each phrasal verb. These meanings are often extensions from the core meaning and they may be abstract. You should study the sentences carefully to see how each phrasal verb is used. Some hints on the meaning are given next to each sentence.

Collocations. Each meaning of a phrasal verb is usually associated with a set of particular words (collocates) within the sentence. For example, *complaints* is a collocate of *deal with*, as in the sentence *we had to deal with a lot of complaints*. Studying the sentences will help you learn these very important word associations. Also the collocate *complaints* provides a clue to the appropriate meaning of *deal with*.

Idioms. Phrasal verbs are often used in idioms such as the expression *look at the big picture*. We include a number of idiomatic uses in this book

Each unit concentrates on one phrasal verb (e.g., *go out*). The phrasal verb is introduced in a table format that (a) highlights the grammar of the phrasal verb, (b) defines its most common meanings, and (c) provides examples of how the phrasal verb is used in everyday English. The information in the table is brief, easy-to-follow, and can be consulted at any time for quick reference. Studying these tables will help you to learn American English as it is used in everyday situations.

Each table is followed by a series of exercises intended to check your understanding of the meaning and uses of the phrasal verb presented in the unit. The exercises generally progress from controlled practice to more open-ended exercises. A wide variety of question types are used; including, fill-in-the-blanks, multiple choice, crossword puzzles, sentence matching, and re-writing, as well as pattern identification, concordance-based research, error correction, and discussion.

Following every four units, you will find a short set of comprehensive review exercises dealing with the phrasal verbs from the previous four chapters. You will also find a key to all of the exercises at the end of the book, which you can use to check your answers. The index contains a list of a list of the phrasal verbs and collocations used in he book.

We hope that you will enjoy **finding out** more about everyday phrasal verbs by **going through** this book step by step, and feel challenged as you **deal with** the information and **work out** answers to the exercises. **Believe in** yourself and really **get into** it! Who knows where you might **end up**?

CONTENTS

UNIT 1: LOOK AT someone/something

STUDY THESE SENTENCES

abc

He **looked at** me for a few seconds.	1	**Basic meaning** = turn eyes toward
Just look at those million-dollar houses!		
	2	**Extended meanings**
The policeman **looked at** my drivers license.		(a) **read quickly, look through**
The study **looked at** 350 patients.		(b) **examine, study, consider**

IDIOMS

*Alan, let's **look at the big picture**.*	3	**look at the big picture** = consider the whole situation
Look at Jeff. He didn't finish college and now he's unemployed.	4	**look at someone/something** = point out someone as an example of something
*It's **not much to look at**, is it?*	5	**not much to look at** = unattractive

EXERCISES

A. **Using the information above, decide which use of** *look at* **is illustrated in each of the following examples.**

1. The whole class was looking at me.   __1__
2. The report looked at smoking trends among teenagers.   _____
3. Look at Asia today. Its economy is booming.   _____
4. Have you had a chance to look at the book yet?   _____
5. He looked at my name tag.   _____
6. The important thing is to look at the big picture.   _____
7. The boat isn't much to look at, but it's all mine.   _____

B. **Draw a line between the two halves to complete the sentence.**

1. The panel will look	at it as an investment.
2. Most people look	at both sides of the tax issue.
3. The way we look	at question number 4.
4. We stopped to look	at fashion is about to change.
5. Let's go to page 2 and look	at a car for sale.

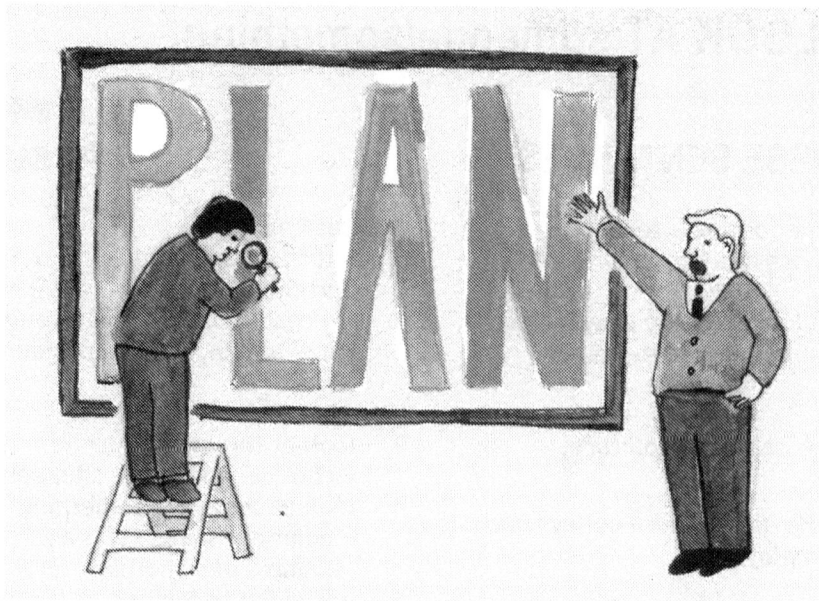

*You've got to **look at** the big picture!*

C. Complete the sentences with a suitable form of *look at* (e.g., *is looking at*) and one of the words or phrases from the box. Be sure to use the correct article (e.g. *a/the*) with the noun where required:

| average family   computer   magazines   sales figures   it   problem |

1. I always .... and try to solve it step by step.
2. If you .... with two kids, they would pay about $400 in higher taxes.
3. The accountant .... for July.
4. He picked up the gold coin and .... carefully.
5. I am always .... in the bookstore.
6. He often .... to check for new email.

D. Complete the dialogues in an appropriate way using *look at*:

1.

Has the President made up his mind whether or not to sign it?

He is ....
....

2.

I have a rash on my back

Is it serious? Maybe you should have a doctor ....
....

8

Unit 2: DEAL WITH someone/something

STUDY THESE SENTENCES

abc

I could no longer **deal with** his outrageous behavior.	1	handle
After selling some bad food, the shop had to **deal with** a lot of complaints.		
The guidelines **deal with** topics such as diet and exercise.	2	cover, be concerned with
Her newspaper articles often **dealt with** problems at work.		
Men are much easier to **deal with** as clients.	3	do business with
We'll continue to **deal with** the Russian government.		

IDIOMS
*Just **deal with** it!*

4   deal with it
=stop making excuses and do something to change a situation

EXERCISES

A. In which of these situations might you tell somebody to *just deal with it*?

1. When you are having a discussion or an argument.
2. When you are trying to be polite.

B. Using the information above, decide which use of *deal with* is illustrated in each of the following examples:

1. Some companies only deal with very wealthy people. _____
2. The company has to find ways to deal with the drop in sales. _____
3. The student says, okay, I can deal with this. _____
4. Her advice column usually deals with relationship problems and how to solve them. _____
5. Government ministers met to talk about how to deal with weapons of mass destruction. _____

C. Fill in the blanks with a correct form of *deal with*:

1. The neighbors are going to have a tough time .... those people.
2. There was a recognition that corruption is a problem and that it has to be ....

9

3. The translators have .... thousands of pages of documents.

4. In my field of work, you .... a wide variety of issues.

D. Complete the sentences with a suitable form of *deal with* (e.g., *is dealing with*) and one of the words from the box. Be sure to use the correct article (e.g. a/the) with the noun where required:

happier	study	techniques	everyone	planning

1. Here are some .... to .... unwanted email.

2. With proper ...., you can .... student loan repayments.

3. .... offers strategies for .... stress.

4. People .... depression often wish for .... days.

5. You cannot .... impossible people the same way you .... else.

E. Discussion questions

1. How do you deal with telemarketers?

2. What is your advice for dealing with the stress of everyday life?

*You can **deal with** this customer!*

Unit 3: DO WITH something

STUDY THESE SENTENCES

abc

She loved anything to **do with** sports.

The changeable weather has something to **do with** global warming.

Mark says he wants **nothing to do with** stolen merchandise.

1   **connected with, related to**

EXPLANATION	
Examples	Meteorologists say that the changeable weather has **something to do with** global warming.
Meaning	Global warming is connected to the changeable weather, but meteorologists are not sure exactly how.
Examples	Marty's surgery had **nothing to do with** his death.
Meaning	The fact that Marty had surgery did not contribute to his death.
CORPUS NOTE:	Strong pattern: ... have nothing/something/anything to do with ... ... has to do with ...

EXERCISES

A. Which possible conclusions can be drawn from the following questions or statements? Choose all that apply:

1. Why does he want nothing to do with his brothers?

    (a) He needs them.
    (b) He is angry with them.
    (c) He wants to be alone.
    (d) He is pleased with his brothers.

2. I just want to tell you that I had nothing to do with the accident.

    (a) I was in an accident.
    (b) I caused the accident.
    (c) I was nowhere near the accident.
    (d) I was not involved in the accident.

3. The future of the city has less to do with business than it has to do with people.

    (a) The future of the city has more to do with people than it has to do with business.
    (b) People play a vital role in the future of the city.
    (c) The future of the city is not connected to business.
    (d) Business is important; however, people are more important.

4. If I have anything to do with it, she will be there.

    (a) She listens to me.
    (b) I don't want to help.
    (c) I will be able to influence her to go.
    (d) I am not involved in the situation.

5.   *A: I'm divorced.*
    B: What's that got to do with anything?

    (a) Speaker B thinks that being divorced is relevant to the topic of conversation.
    (b) Speaker B thinks that being divorced is irrelevant to the topic of conversation.

B. Choose an appropriate word from the box to best complete the sentences:

attack	show business	report	robbery	upbringing
	weight training		share prices	

1. The defendant said he had nothing to do with the.. .
2. She said her success had to do with ....
3. The film star enjoys relaxing with her husband, who has nothing to do with

    ....
4. The army denied that it had anything to do with the ....
5. The high price of oil has little to do with the drop in ....
6. His attitude had a lot to do with his ....
    in Texas.
7. I have a question. It has to do with the overall goal of the ....

*Is it something **to do with** music?*

12

Unit 4:GO BACK to somewhere/something

STUDY THESE SENTENCES

We're **going back** to California in June. After eating breakfast, she **went back** to bed.	1	**return (to a place)**
The use of personal computers **goes back** to the eighties. Her career in show business **went back** to 1947.	2	**date back** (= the use of personal computers started in the eighties)
He **went back** to school to finish his degree. *I want to go back to something that John said.*	3	**return** (to a situation or topic or activity)

IDIOMS

We need to go back to square one *We need to go back to the drawing board*	4	**go back to square one** = we need to start from the beginning
We go way back/go back a long way.	5	**go back a long way** = we've known each other for a long time

RELATED PHRASAL VERB **go back on** your word/promise/agreement	**go back on** =not do what you said you would do

EXERCISES

A. Using the information above, decide which use of *go back* is illustrated in each of the following examples:

1. His proposal was to go back to the previous voting system. _____
2. Her involvement in the museum goes back 10 years. _____
3. You have to go back a long way. _____
4. Some farmers are going back to traditional farming methods. _____
5. John Glenn wanted to go back into space. _____

B. Study the following sentences:

1. After losing the game, the coach said that they would just have to **go back to the drawing board**.
2. The new plan is not working and so we have to **go back to the drawing board**.

Question: Do these sentences share a similar meaning? In your own words, explain what it means to *go back to the drawing board*. What is another way of saying this?

C. **Draw a line between the two halves of each sentence. There may be more than one set of correct answers.**

1. He went
2. There's no going
3. We could go
4. Her involvement in the museum goes
5. The employers and unions will have to go

back to where we were.
back to the negotiating table.
back 10 years.
back and see what she said.
back to school to finish his degree.

D. **Discussion question**

1. Where is the most beautiful place you have ever visited? Would you like to go back there someday?

2. If you could go back in time, which era would you visit? What would you do?

Okay, we have to go back to the drawing board again.

Unit 5: REVIEW
LOOK AT, DEAL WITH, DO WITH, GO BACK

A. Fill in the blanks with an appropriate phrasal verb. Be sure to use the correct form of the verb:

1. A. Did he contact you by mail on the 4th or 6th April?
   B. I'd have .... and .... the letter.

2. A: Women who are getting a divorce shouldn't go to a woman lawyer
   B: I don't think gender has anything .... it.

3. Dr. Johnson will lecture on topics .... diet and exercise.

4. The politician claimed that he had nothing .... the decision.

5. We're trying to move the start date. In the interim, we are ....
   other options.

B. Rewrite the underlined parts of the sentences using the correct phrasal verb:

1. The government is <u>considering</u> different strategies for meeting greenhouse gas targets.

2. If you can't <u>handle</u> the heat, get out of the kitchen.

3. The cake's delicious taste <u>is due to</u> the high quality of chocolate used in the recipe.

4. After she <u>examined</u> everything that's in the booklet, she still had real concerns.

5. His controversial book <u>covers</u> the final hours of Princess Diana's life.

6. You are <u>facing</u> 5 years in prison.

7. He has had a good track record <u>over the last</u> several years.

C. Read the following sentences and decide which people are experiencing negative feelings and which are experiencing positive feelings:

1. Stop trying to blame me. I had nothing to do with it.
2. John really doesn't deal with his problems very well.
3. I can't believe I get to go back and see her again.
4. I can't believe I have to go back and see her again.
5. Wow! Just look at those waves!

15

6. It has been a pleasure dealing with your company.

7. Right now I'm looking at all of the destruction and I can't believe my eyes.

D. Each of the sentences below contains an error with a phrasal verb. Cross out the incorrect word and write the correct word on the line:

1. The mayor has nothing to do on education policy.   _____

2. His criminal record goes back to 10 years.   _____

3. She loves anything to do for cooking.   _____

4. You have to look about a job and decide if it is what you want.   _____

5. Our firm will continue to deal to the Fortune 500 companies.   _____

6. I think we are looking in sometime mid-morning for the meeting.   _____

7. Sara and Jack just got back for their vacation in the Bahamas.   _____

8. The guidelines deal about topics such as health and welfare.   _____

*Is it something to **do with** birds?*

Unit 6: COME UP

STUDY THESE SENTENCES

abc

Marilyn **came up** two flights of stairs to my apartment.	1	**Basic meaning:** movement
She had **come up** from Houston for the event.		(a) from a lower physical (geographical) location to a higher location
People **come up** to me to ask for my autograph.		(b) toward somebody or something (=approach)
The winter has been so mild that the tulips are already starting to **come up** in the yard.	2	**Extended meanings:** (a) emerge/rise/appear = appear
After Windows **comes up** on the screen, the computer freezes.		
The election is **coming up** in November.		= take place in the future
Mr. Thompson has **come up** quickly through the organization to become CEO.		= advance/be promoted at work
She has certainly **come up** in the world since her days as a waitress.		
Did my name **come up** in the meeting?		(b) mentioned/discussed in conversation
The question of money never **came up** again.		
I won't be able to make the meeting; something's **come up**.		(c) happened unexpectedly

IDIOMS

The police **came up empty-handed** in their search for the suspect.	3	**come up empty-handed** = to not find something or to be unsuccessful in something you are doing
The company wanted to take over the bank, but had **come up short** with its $12 billion offer.	4	**come up short** = close to reaching a goal, but unsuccessful; fail to reach a goal

RELATED PHRASAL VERBS

The consultants **came up with** a plan to save the company.	5	**come up with** think of a plan/proposal/idea
A New York businessman has four weeks **to come up with** $4 million..		get a particular sum of money
The industry is **coming up against** angry protesters.	6	= facing or running into difficult problems/people

17

EXERCISES

A. **Using the information above, decide which use of** *come up* **is illustrated in each of the following examples:**

1. Your performance review is coming up in March.   _____
2. I imagine that the panel will come up with several recommendations.   _____
3.   At 36, he has come up quickly through the organization to become president.
    _____
4. John's name comes up as a possible future leader.   _____
5. Sometimes people come up to you in the street and ask for money.   _____
6. I made a list of points that came up a number of times.   _____
7. Slow down a bit because we're coming up on Lawrence Ave. on the left. _____
8. If my numbers come up, we'll be rich!   _____

B. **Draw a line between the two halves of each sentence.**

1. The government failed to come up	something's come up.
2. The chip industry is coming up	with a solution to the problem.
3. We should encourage students to guess	around 6 a.m.
4. We thought we could win the game,	against fierce competition.
5. I won't be able to go to the movie;	if they can't come up with an answer.
6. The sun comes up	but we came up short.

C. **Select the best answer(s) to fill in the blanks:**

1. A person who is able to come up with lots of great ideas is probably somebody _____.

    (a) creative
    (b) lazy
    (c) mean
    (d) heartbroken

2. **If you've** *come up against a brick wall*, **then it means** _____.

    (a) you've crashed your car
    (b) you can't make any progress
    (c) you're a procrastinator
    (d) you lay bricks for a living

3. Somebody who comes up quickly through an organization to become a top executive is probably _____.

   (a) an underachiever
   (b) a hard-worker
   (c) ambitious
   (d) motivated

4. Clare told Steve, "John came up to see me yesterday". Which of the following statements could be true?

   (a) Clare lives in an apartment building.
   (b) John drove north to see Clare.
   (c) John's house is located south of Clare's house.
   (d) John lives on the floor above Clare.

D. Discussion Questions

   1. Your friend tells you that *something's come up* and he can't go out tonight. List three possible reasons why he might say this (e.g. he hasn't finished his homework).

   2. Imagine that you were a celebrity. How would you feel if fans were constantly coming up to you and asking for pictures or an autograph?

   3. At what age should you come up with a plan for your retirement?

   4. What holidays are coming up on the calendar?

   5. If you had to come up with an idea for a new product, what would it be?

Unit 7: GO ON

STUDY THESE SENTENCES

💬 ●●●●●
abc ●●●●●

OTHER PATTERNS go on (to) something; go on ahead

As time **goes on**, things will get better.	1	continue
The negotiations **went on** for two years.		carry on
A bidding war is **going on** between Boeing and Airbus.	2	occur, happen, take place
The residents were angry about what was **going on** in their community.		
Tom Cruise **went on** to star in many more blockbuster movies.	3	move on, continue
Can we go on to page 10?		
Frank **went on (and on)** about how much money he could have saved.	4	talk excessively, complain
Coach Wallace **went on** the local news to talk about the team's recent loss.	5	appear on TV/radio

IDIOMS

Go on, have another scoop of ice-cream.	6	**go on!** = informal way to encourage somebody to do something
She needed to **go on** Ritalin to control ADD.	7	**go on drugs** = begin to take medication
He told me to **go on ahead** and that he'd catch up to me later.	8	**go on ahead** = start walking/driving

EXERCISES

A. Using the information above, decide which use of *go on* is illustrated in each of the following examples:

    1. The president is due to go on Iranian TV.   ____

    2. After graduation, he went on to win a major tournament.   ____

    3. The effort to improve the local environment has gone on for a few years.

                                                             ____

    4. The American people see what is going on and they don't like it.   ____

    5. I'll go on ahead and buy us tickets.   ____

B. Complete the sentences with a suitable form of *go on* (e.g., *is going on*) and one of the words from the box. Be sure to use the correct article (e.g. *a/the*) with the noun where required:

| upset | list | news program | electrician | discussion | world |

1. The younger brother .... to study electronics and worked as ....
2. Last night, the company's spokesperson .... ABC's ....
3. There is a lively .... between those in favor of the changes and those who oppose the changes.
4. He isn't ...., but that's because he doesn't really know what's ....
5. What in the .... here?
6. We'll add to .... as we ....

C. Complete the dialogues in an appropriate way using *go on*:

1. A: *Do you think we'll have a chance to talk about this issue again?*
   B: *I'm sure there will be some more meetings* ....

2. A: *Why did the conference run so late tonight?*
   B: *Unfortunately the speeches* ....

3. A: .... *at work?*
   B: *The usual. My boss orders me around a lot and I'm expected to work weekends now, too.*

4. A: *How long has the team been working to restore the sculpture to its original condition?*
   B: .... *for roughly three years now.*

D. Discussion Questions

How would you deal with:
1. a boss who goes on and on about how much he dislikes the city?
2. a relative who has gone on medication, but refuses to take it regularly?
3. a girlfriend who dreams of leaving her office job to go on to a modeling career?
4. an argument with a close friend that has gone on for over a week?
5. being chosen to go on TV to star in a new reality show?

Unit 8: COME BACK

STUDY THESE SENTENCES

Sally will **come back** to Seattle for the holidays.	1	a. return (from a place)
Ponchos are **coming back** in style.		b. return to popularity/fashion synonym: make a comeback
His confidence is starting to **come back**	2	return, restart
Details about the accident **came back** to her after she visited the site.	3	remember (suddenly)
I wish I could have **come back** with a smart remark to Jack's comment about my haircut.	4	reply with a quick, appropriate remark

EXERCISES

A. For each sentence below give the correct form of *come back* (e.g. *coming back*), then decide if the meaning of *come back* is *return, restart, remember*, or *reply* and write the answer on the line.

1. Store owners are hoping that advertising will encourage shoppers .... to the mall. _____

2. The issue .... to the point John was making. _____

3. It took hours, but the power finally .... on around noon. _____

4. (Looking at a photo) It's all .... to me now! _____

B. Using your own words, explain the meaning of the following sentences:

1. In the end, her words came back to haunt her.

2. Her husband went to war and never came back.

3. Luckily the diabetes test came back negative.

4. Sandy has worked hard to come back from an elbow injury.

C. Complete the following dialogue between two friends:

1. A: .... ?
   B: *We plan to stay in Atlanta until Sunday and come back here early Monday.*

2. A: ....?
   B: *Right now I am very excited, but tomorrow I'll have to come back down to earth. I have a ton of packing to do!*
3. A: *I bet.*
   B: ....
4. A: *Well, I hope you come back full of energy after your vacation.*
   B: ....

*I thought bowties had **come back in style***

D. Describe a scenario where each of the following situations occurs. Provide as many details as you can:

1. a creature comes back to life

2. a team comes back to win the game

3. your words come back to haunt you

4. a skier comes back with a bronze medal

5. an old toy comes back in style

6. somebody yells, "Don't ever come back".

Unit 9: WORK ON something/someone

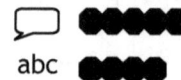

STUDY THESE SENTENCES

NASA is **working on** a new rocket.

1 spend time on something

She has been **working on** me to join her volunteer group

2 try to persuade someone to do something

IDIOMS

I'm **working on the assumption** that he was intoxicated at the time of the offense..

3 **working on the assumption** = rely on an idea/assumption being true when developing ones own ideas or plans

EXERCISES

A. Draw a line between the two halves of each sentence.

1. The student became interested in working
2. The pharmaceutical company has been working
3. The architect is working
4. The psychiatrist suggested he work
5. Scientists must be immunized before working
6. We had been working
7. The chairperson was working

on a new design for a skyscraper.
on improving his self-esteem.

on drugs to reduce blood pressure.
on dangerous viruses.
on them to change their policy.

on the idea that we'd reach an agreement this week.
on nuclear physics.

B. Create full sentences with an appropriate form of *work on* using the words provided in the brackets. The first one has been done for you.

1. (popular singer/new solo album)
   The popular singer is working on a new solo album.

2. (company/correcting the problem)

   ....

3. (veterinarian/sick or injured animals)

   ....

4. (author/currently/novel set in Las Vegas)

....

5. (mathematician/calculus problem/prove a theory)

....

6. (teacher/students/do their homework)

....

7. (I/assumption/meeting will take place very soon)

....

C. Discussion Questions

1. Have you ever had to really work on somebody to convince him/her of something?
   What was it?
   Were you successful?

2. What kind of tasks or projects do you work on that require a lot of time and effort?

I have to work on the accounts

Unit 10: REVIEW
COME UP, GO ON, COME BACK, WORK ON

A. Complete the sentences with the correct form of the verb in parentheses and one of the following particles (*up, on, back*).

1. You'll need to be creative in order to .... (come) with some new ideas.
2. I need to rest for a while, but you should .... (go) ahead. I'll catch up.
3. After restarting the computer, Windows XP doesn't ....(come) on the screen.
4. I wonder what would happen if the boat didn't .... (come) to get us.
5. After the semifinals, the team .... (go) to win the championship title.
6. My colleague .... (come) with a proposal for improving our performance.
7. The writer has been .... (work) Reagan's biography for ten years.
8. The American people see what is .... (go) and they don't like it.

B. Answer yes or no to the following questions about phrasal verbs:

1. If something **comes up**, did you expect it to happen?
2. If you hear that, "a trial is **going on** in Chicago", is the trial happening right now?
3. If you **come up** to somebody's apartment, are you visiting on the ground floor?
4. If somebody **went on** to do great things, did they always do great things?
5. If your involvement in a project **goes back** five years, are you still involved in the project?
6. If you **came back** to see someone, were you visiting for the first time?
7. If you read that, "the effort to improve the local environment has **gone on** for a few years", does this mean that the effort has continued?
8. If somebody **comes up** to you on the street, are they far away?
9. If your name **came up** in conversation, was it mentioned?
10. If you **went back** to Hollywood in June, had you been there before?
11. If you have been **working on** a project for 6 months, is the project finished?
12. If somebody **went on** about something, did they talk about it briefly?

C. Correct the errors in these sentences. There is one error in each sentence.

1. I'll come up to this topic in a minute.
2. We thought we could win the competition, but we came up tall.
3. As time goes back, things will get better.
4. He didn't like the dorm, so he gone back to live with his grandmother.
5. Our plan didn't work out and so now we have to go on to square one.

Unit 11: GO THROUGH something

STUDY THESE SENTENCES

💬 ●●●●●
abc ●●●

She was **going through** a divorce and was depressed.	1	**undergo or experience** something (usually unpleasant)
All teams **go through** periods of bad luck. The company expects the deal to **go through**.	2	**succeed** agreements and laws go through
This route takes a little longer, but **goes through** some magnificent scenery..	3	**passes through**
He **went through** his father's papers.	4	**sort out/organize**
The circus animals **go through** 5 tons of hay and 750 pounds of carrots each week.	5	**use, eat**

IDIOMS

When I heard the news, several thoughts **went through** my mind..	6	**go through my mind**
Real estate prices are about to **go through the roof**.	7	**go through the roof** =increase (dramatically)

RELATED PHRASAL VERB

Julie decided that she just wasn't ready to **go through with** the wedding.	8	**go through with** something =go ahead with something, usually difficult

EXERCISES

A. **Using the information above, decide which use of** *go through* **is illustrated in each of the following examples:**

1. Not eating vegetables is a phase that most toddlers go through. ____
2. Let me go through what we have done up to this point. ____
3. He may leave the company if the reorganization plan goes through. ____
4. I went through ten different contractors on this job. ____
5. His shot went through the legs of the goalkeeper. ____
6. For the final episode of Friends, the ratings went through the roof. ____
7. I knew what was going through her head. ____
8. He won't go through with the chemotherapy. ____

B. **Study the patterns below then add to the lists:**

(a) go through X
   -a divorce
   -a mid life crisis

(b) X go through the roof
   -prices
   -inflation

27

-a tough time   -ratings

_____   _____

_____   _____

<u>(c) go through with X</u>   <u>(d) go through X</u>
   -a plan   -papers
-    -an adoption   -tax returns
-    -a lawsuit   -the attic

   _____   _____

   _____   _____

C. Complete the sentences with a suitable form of *go through* (e.g., *is going through*) and
    one of the words from the box. Be sure to use the correct article (e.g. a/the) with the
    noun where required:

mind	life	interest rates	mid-life crisis	closet	attorneys

    1. My friend, who was .... , bought a new sports car.
    2. The government raised .... to stop inflation from
       .... the roof.
    3. I need to .... and decide which old clothes I want to donate.
    4. What .... as you watched that film clip?
    5. We .... three .... on this
       case before we finally settled it.
    6. Nobody wants to .... alone.

D. Discussion Questions
    1. Have you ever helped somebody who was
       going through a difficult time?
    2. How long does it take you to go through
       a gallon of milk?
       a dozen eggs?
       a block of cheese?
       a box of chocolates?
    3. What typically goes through your mind as
       you watch the news?
    4. What type of training do you have to go
       through for your job?

Profits are going through the roof!

Unit 12: GET INTO something

STUDY THESE SENTENCES

Some music fans tried to **get into** the concert without paying. | 1 | enter a place
You get paid a lot of money when you **get into** pro sports | 2 | involve oneself in
She was hoping to **get into** Harvard. | 3 | join an organization
I put on weight and had trouble **getting into** my clothes. | 4 | put on (clothes)

IDIOMS

Martha Stewart was doing well, but then **she got into trouble with the law..** | 5 | **get into trouble**
get into a difficult situation
While he was in college, **he got into drugs** | 6 | **get into** something
get into a habit/a routine
He was acting strangely and I wondered **what had gotten into him.** | 7 | something **has gotten into** someone
= something is making him behave strangely

EXERCISES

A. Using the information above, decide which use of *get into* is illustrated in each of the following examples:

1. I made my classmates laugh at school and that's how I got into comedy.

2. John and Pat got into an argument over money. _____
3. Keep playing well and you will get into the tournament. _____
4. If you have bad grades, it is almost impossible to get into the top colleges. _____
5. Gary will get into this in more detail. _____

B. Complete the sentences with a suitable form of *get into* (e.g., *getting into*) and one of the words from the box. Be sure to use the correct article (e.g. *a/the*) with the noun where required:

| national press   inspectors   American waterways   MBA program   industry |

1. There was a report today saying that ....
North Korea as early as January.

29

2. He .... with the idea of making movies like "It's a Wonderful Life."
3. An estimated half-billion gallons of oil .... every year.
4. You can trace how this story ....
5. She was really hoping ....

I hope I can get into Harvard Business School.

C. Discussion Questions

1. Have you recently gotten into a bad habit or routine that you'd like to break?

2. Did you ever get into trouble for something you didn't do?

3. Was there ever a time when you noticed that somebody was acting strangely and wondered what had gotten into them? Explain the situation.

4. What new hobby or leisure activity would you seriously consider getting into?

5. If you want to get into a good school, what should you do?

Unit 13: FIND OUT something; FIND something OUT

STUDY THESE SENTENCES

OTHER PATTERNS find out what/that ...
I want to **find out** how much the new DVD players cost.

Doing business in that country is not always easy; my company **found** that **out**.

1 discover
(a) (find out something)
(b) (find something out)

EXERCISES

A. Complete the sentences with the correct form of *find* and the particle *out*. If there is one blank space, then write the verb and particle together.

1. Traveling abroad can be difficult. The Jones family .... (find) that .... when they visited Iceland.

2. I can't answer it now, but I'll see if I can .... (find).

3. We .... (find) we ran out of time.

4. It is the job of reporters to .... (find) things ....

5. Did you take the time to .... if they had insurance?

B. Study the following sentences:
1.
(a) The first step is to find out what is really going on here
(b) Take this quiz and find out how much you know about films
(c) The police wanted to find out who saw the accident
(d) Did you take the time to find out if they had insurance?
(e) We'll find that out when she gets here.

2. What patterns do you observe in the sentences above? Explain your observations below:

_____

3. Using your own words, write two sentences that follow the same pattern you recognized above:

31

(a) ....
(b) ....

C. Study the patterns below then add to the lists:

(a) find out X
- the answer
- who your friends are

_____
_____
_____

(b) find out what...
- happened
- is going on here

_____
_____
_____

(c) find out if...
- he had read the book
- anyone had seen anything

_____
_____
_____

(d) find out how...
- much he understood
- to put the desk together

_____
_____
_____

D. Discussion Questions

Find out new information.   Use the newspaper or web to answer these questions:

1. If you need to find out today's weather, check here:

   ....

2. If you want to find out how your stocks are doing, look here

   ....

3. If you're a sports fan and want to find out if your favorite baseball team won their game last night, go here:

   ....

4. If you need to find something out about buying a computer, you should look here:

   ....

5. If you're looking to find out about the latest designer fashions, try here:

   ....

Unit 14: SET UP something

STUDY THESE SENTENCES

💬 ●●●●
abc ●●●●

OTHER PATTERNS set someone/something up, be set up

The Red Cross **set up** a temporary shelter for the homeless.	**1**	**build/put up a structure**
He **set up** a meeting with his boss to discuss his ideas.	**2**	**plan/schedule/establish something**

IDIOMS

Ray says that he was **set up** by a man he met in a bar.	**3**	**set** someone **up/set up** someone/ be **set up** by someone = make somebody appear guilty of doing something wrong/illegal
They seemed compatible, so **I set them up.**	**4**	**set them up** = arrange for two people to meet with the hope of starting a romantic relationship

EXERCISES

A. Complete the sentences with the correct form of the verb *set*. If there is one blank space in the sentence, write the verb and particle there; if there are two blank spaces, write the correct form of the verb in the first space and the particle *up* in the second one:

1. He has already made enough money .... (set) himself .... for life.

2. They contacted the creditors and .... (set) a payment plan.

3. Aviana is .... (set) a low-cost airline called Egg.

4. The state is aiming .... (set) a job-training program for high school dropouts.

5. I hope he's not .... (set) himself .... for failure.

33

B. Draw a line between the two halves of each sentence.

1. The insurance companies   set up a stand to sell lemonade.
2. The Spacewatch program was   set up.
3. The Internet Connection Wizard   set up to monitor the sky for
                                        asteroids.
4. The city is   set up a payment plan.
5. They contact the creditors and   set up mobile offices in Florida.
6. The children   setting up a telephone hotline.
7. There is no doubt that he was   set up my Internet connection.

C. What do you think the following phrases mean? Verify your answers with the help of a dictionary then use your own words to write a sentence using each phrase:

1. Set up shop
meaning:
....
sentence:
....

2. Set up camp
meaning:
....
sentence:
....

3. Set up house
meaning:
....
sentence:
....

D. Discussion Questions

1. Have you ever set up your own website?   If not, do you know somebody who could do the job?
2. Can you recall the plot of a book or movie in which somebody was set up? Briefly explain what happened.
3. Tell whether you agree or disagree with the following statement, "a good education sets you up for life".
4. Have you ever been set up on a blind date? If so, what was the outcome?   Have you ever set someone up on a blind date?   If yes, what was the outcome? If not, would you like to play matchmaker one day?

Unit 15: REVIEW
GO THROUGH, GET INTO, FIND OUT, SET UP

A. Using complete sentences, answer these questions about the phrasal verbs examined in units 11-14:

1. If prices go through the roof, are they considered lower or higher than normal?
2. If you're wondering what has gotten into your brother is it because he is acting normally or strangely?
3. If you just found out the price of the car that you're interesting in buying, do you know how much it costs?
4. If somebody just went through a divorce, are they still married?
5. If your friend got into law school, was she accepted?
6. If you set up a meeting with a colleague, did you schedule it or cancel it?
7. If a government bill was passed, did it go through?
8. If the police have witnesses to the accident, does this mean they found out who saw it?
9. If a chef finishes every bag of flour that he has in order to bake cakes for his restaurant, does he go through all of the flour?
10. If you went through with the plan, did you do it?

B. Replace the underlined word or phrase with the appropriate phrasal verb or idiomatic phrase:

1. Mary organized her father's papers before bringing them to the accountant.
2. You don't want to experience the rest of your life alone.
3. She was hoping to join the Junior League.
4. The draft has undergone a number of revisions.
5. I don't know how deeply we can become involved in that.
6. The company can expect to face tougher environmental regulations.
7. In their early research, the scientists did not find what they were searching for.

C. Correct the errors in these sentences. There is one error in each sentence.

1. After working for a large company for many years, he set up himself as an independent consultant.
2. I knew what was going up her head.
3. The government raised interest rates to stop inflation from going out the roof.
4. The president is set up a North America Free Trade Association.
5. Route 89 goes into some incredible scenery.

D. Fill in the blanks of the sentences below to complete the word puzzle:

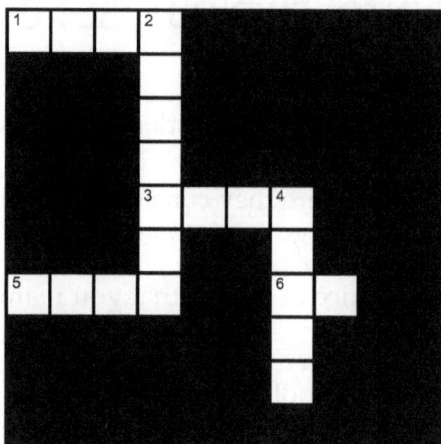

Across:
1. You can use the instrument to ___ out what your heart rate is.
3. The show's ratings went through the ___.
5. The company set ___ a trust fund in the Cayman Islands.
6. They knew that they would ___ up against a variety of obstacles.

Down:
2. David was going through a tough ___.
4. I ___ out how simple it was to get a job in Detroit

I want to set up a business

Unit 16: COME OUT of something

STUDY THESE SENTENCES

abc

OTHER PATTERNS: come out of somewhere, come out that ...

He **came out** of the elevator with a couple of friends.	1	leave (a room, building etc.)
The story **came out** that the CEO had threatened to resign.	2	release, make public (reports/info/feelings, etc.)
The president **came out** firmly in support of military action.	3	publicly show support for/against something
The senator **came out** against the Republican party resolution.		

IDIOMS

The singer **came out of nowhere** and sold three million copies.	4	come out of nowhere = appear suddenly or when least expected
The Mets are hoping to **come out on top** at the end of the season.	5	come out on top = be successful; win

EXERCISES

A. Using the information above, decide which use of *come out* is illustrated in each of the following examples:

1. It came out that the politician had received money from the oil company.

    ____

2. He didn't think he was going to come out of prison alive.

    ____

3. When the evidence comes out at trial, my client's good name will be restored.

    ____

4. The chairman came out against the decision.

    ____

5. There is no guarantee that good managers will come out on top.   ____

6. It is unlikely that an unknown actor will come out of nowhere to win the award.

    ____

B. Complete the sentences with a suitable form of *come out* (e.g., *is coming out*) and one of the words from the box. Be sure to use the correct article (e.g. a/the) with the noun where required:

plan	sales reports	series	court
initiatives		kitchen	retirement

1. Ten minutes later he .... of .... with a chicken sandwich.
2. The ex-CEO of the company had to .... of ....
3. We were surprised by .... that .... today.
4. "The facts of the case will .... in ....," the lawyer said.
5. The chairman of the board .... squarely against ....
6. The publisher has .... with .... of mini-books.
7. People are expecting the government to .... with some new .... next month.

C. Study the patterns below then add to the lists. Use a dictionary, if necessary.

1.

(a) come out of X	(b) come out with X	(c) X came out
- a slump	- a series of books	- the story
- retirement	- new initiatives	- the truth
_____	_____	_____
_____	_____	_____
_____	_____	_____

2. Explain what the following phrases mean. Use a dictionary, if necessary:

come out of the closet, come out in droves, come out ahead

D. Discussion Questions

1. Describe a situation where you or someone you know really came out on top.

2. Do you think it is common for a person to come out of retirement? Can you name a famous person who has come out of retirement (e.g. sports celebrities)? In your opinion, was this a wise decision for that person to make?

Unit 17: FIGURE OUT something

STUODY THESE SENTENCES

abc

OTHER PATTERNS figure someone out, figure out what/that ....
I still haven't **figured out** all the rules.   1   understand, work out
The police are trying to **figure out** what   find out
 happened.

EXERCISES

A. Complete the sentences with a suitable form of *figure out* (e.g., *is figuring out*) and one
   of the words from the box. Be sure to use the correct article (e.g. a/the) with the
   noun where required:

rules	home	solution	tax	customers	wreckage

1. It doesn't take a rocket scientist to ....
2. I still haven't .... all ....
3. Gazing at ...., he said he was still trying to
   .... how it happened.
4. We must .... how much .... we owe.
5. We owe it to our .... how we can do a better job.
6. He was trying to .... how to get us .... safely.

B. Draw a line between the two halves of each sentence. There is more than one correct
   answer for each. How many different combinations can you make?

1. I am sure Sandy can figure   out why my computer keeps crashing.
2. I'm trying to figure   out that being famous has its drawbacks.
3. Some companies have figured   out what the economy will be like next
                                             year.
4. It didn't take me long to figure   out a way to do it.
5. Everyone is trying to figure   out how to avoid paying state taxes.

C. Study the patterns below then add to the lists:

(a) figure out X   **(b) figure out what X...**
- a solution   - happened
_____   _____
_____   _____
_____   _____

39

(c) figure out why X...
- my computer keeps crashing

_____
_____
_____

(d) figure out how X...
- to get home safely

_____
_____
_____

D. **Discussion Questions**

1. Can you figure out the answers to the exercises in this unit?

2. Are you good at figuring out puzzles like crosswords and sudoku?

3. Could you figure out how to install Windows on your computer?

4. Do you know someone who can figure out business accounting?

5. It takes ten workers six weeks to build a house. Can you figure out how long it would take twelve workers?

6. I can't figure my brother out. Do you know someone who is hard to figure out?

I'm still trying to figure it out.

Unit 18: GO INTO something

STUDY THESE SENTENCES

abc

When I **went into** the bank, I saw the long line of customers.	1	**enter** a location
He decided to **go into** interior design.	2	**enter** a particular job, profession, business
The witnesses **went into** great detail about what they had seen.	3	**describe, talk about** a topic
A lot of work **went into** the planning stage.	4	**time/money/effort put into** something
The airline industry **went into** recession after 9/11.	5	**enter** a state

IDIOMS

When the new law **goes into effect**, smoking will be banned in restaurants.	6	**go into effect** = new rules/laws, etc. officially begin
I **went into shock** after the accident.	7	**go into shock/go into withdrawal/go into debt**

EXERCISES

A. Using the information above, decide which use of *go into* is illustrated in each of the following examples:

1. Every day I watched the office workers go into the building. _____
2. Poor pay may discourage some people from going into nursing. _____
3. All the work that went into it was well worth it. _____
4. After a while the computer goes into a sleep mode. _____
5. The new car tax went into effect in 1998. _____
6. The talks must avoid going into too much detail. _____

B. Create full sentences with an appropriate form of *go into* using the words provided in the brackets. The first one has been done for you.

1. (Wendy / nursing)
   Wendy went into nursing_____.

2. (new satellite system / service last year)
   ....

3. (Ken / decided / business / for himself)
   ....

4. (Since / the early eighties / billions of dollars / research on heart disease)

....

5. (report on pensions / great detail / on the problems / facing many people)

....

C. **Read the following sentences and then answer the questions about them:**

1. The son was encouraged go into the family business.
   Where did the son work?

2. My husband went into construction and worked hard for many years.
   What is the husband's job?

3. Poor pay may discourage some people from going into nursing.
   Do people in the nursing field get paid a lot?

4. Sandra told her parents she wanted to go into show business.
   What does Sandra want to do for a living?

5. Three billion dollars went into the Hubble telescope.
   How much has been invested in the Hubble telescope?

D. **Discussion Questions**

1. What time do you go into work in the morning?

2. If you could belong to any profession other than your own, which profession would go into?

3. When you meet somebody for the first time, how much detail would you go into about your personal life?

4. How would you feel if a new law went into effect that banned drivers from using cell phones while operating their cars?

5. How much time and effort goes into planning a party?

Unit 19: PUT IN something; PUT something IN

STUDY THESE SENTENCES

He **put** a quarter **in** the parking meter.	1	**place** something **in** something
She **puts in** fewer than 100 hours a month at the office.	2	**spend time/effort**
The office manager **put in** an order for 10 new computers.	3	**submit order/request, etc.**
We'll have to remove the old windows and **put in** new ones.	4	**install**

IDIOMS

Sandy was **put in charge of** the West Coast office.	5	**put in charge of** = **make** someone **the head / the leader**
A series of anti-terrorist measures have been **put in place**.	6	**put in place** = **establish**

EXERCISES

A. Using the information above, decide which use of *put in* is illustrated in each of the following examples:

1. Last week I was putting in 15-hour days. _____
2. I went to the bank and put the money in my checking account. _____
3. Every spring she puts in her herbs and flowers. _____
4. We are thinking about putting in a new air conditioner. _____
5. His boss told him to put in his request for a transfer. _____
6. The government plans to revise tax laws that were put in place in 1995.

_____

7. He decided to put the new vice-president in charge of manufacturing.

_____

B. Read the following phrases then use your own words to explain what they mean. Use a dictionary to verify your answers. What types of nouns could you substitute for "it"?

(a) *put it in its simplest form*

....

(b) *put it in those terms*

....

(c) *put it in writing*

....

43

C. **Complete the sentences with the correct form of the verb *put*. If there is one blank space, then write in the space the verb form together with the particle *in*.:**

1. Combine all the ingredients and .... (put) them
.... a casserole dish.

2. Part of the new welfare-to-work program .... (put) place last year.

3. Every spring she .... (put) her herbs and flowers.

4. The news from home .... (put) him ....
a difficult situation.

5. He .... (put) fewer than 100 hours a month at the office.

D. Discussion Questions

1. What kind of situation might require you to put in a lot of hours?

2. What kind of situation might require you to put in a written request for something?

3. Have you ever been put in charge of a large group of people?

4. Have you ever put in for a transfer at work?

Unit 20: REVIEW
COME OUT, FIGURE OUT, GO INTO, PUT IN

A. Using complete sentences, answer these questions about the phrasal verbs examined in units 16-19:

1. If the story came out that the CEO had threatened to resign, was the story publicized?
2. If the senator came out against the Republican party resolution, does s/he agree with it?
3. If the police are trying to figure out what happened, do they already know what happened?
4. "Kelly has been to Egypt many times, but has never gone into the desert."   Has Kelly ever been to the Egyptian desert?
5. "He went into business with his father." Does he work with his father?
6. "A lot of work went into the planning stage." Where was a great deal of time and effort spent?
7. If a new satellite system went into service last year, is it operating now?
8. "All the work that went into it was well worth it." Was the work that went into the project considered a waste of time?
9. "Last month I was putting in 15-hour days." How much time did the person spend at work on a daily basis last month?
10. "He picked up the frog and put it in his pocket." Where is the frog?

B. Replace the underlined word or phrase with the appropriate phrasal verb or idiomatic phrase:

1. The government plans to revise estate laws that were established in 1982.
2. We have to decide what to do with juveniles who commit crimes.
3. When I entered the bank, I saw the long line of customers.
4. He was an actor who wanted to pursue politics.
5. Over the weekend I installed a new front door.
6. I visited the National Gallery and saw some paintings by my favorite artist.
7. It is time to replace the batteries in the radio with new ones.
8. The idea didn't just appear out of thin air.

C. Correct the errors in these sentences. There is one error in each sentence.

1. The dancer came out of everywhere and was very successful.
2. The new service goes into effect last year.
3. I went out the kitchen to get some coffee.
4. It will take us a while to figure up what is going on here.
5. The president came in strongly in support of the action.

D. Complete the word puzzle:

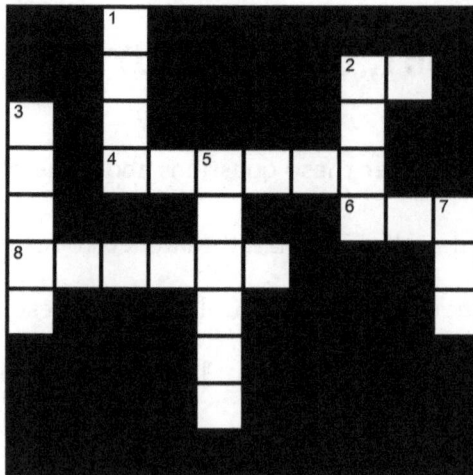

Across

2. There is a possibility that the police put words _____ his mouth.
4. When the new law goes into _____ next fall, all teenagers must be home by 10:30 pm.
6. Cadillac will be coming _____ with its own sports utility vehicle.
8. Sarah was put in _____ of the West Coast office.

Down

1. This is not a new idea that has come out of the _____.
2. He briefly considered going _____ management.
3. They went into _____ after the car accident.
5. I was trying to _____ out how we could do better next time.
7. Naturally, I'd like to come out on _____ at the end of the competition.

I've decided to go into business for myself

Unit 21: GO OUT

STUDY THESE SENTENCES

abc

In China, people often **go out** after dinner.	1	**leave my/your house**
Three months later, she started **going out** with Craig.	2	**have a romantic relationship with**
The advertising brochures will **go out** on May 1.	3	**a letter, etc. being mailed, sent out**
They were trapped in the elevator when the power **went out**.	4	**=power supply fails**

IDIOMS

Every year hundreds of farmers **go out of business**.	5	**go out of business; go bankrupt;** =close a business
The boss **went out of his way** to thank everyone personally.	6	**go out of my way** =make a special effort to do something

EXERCISES

A. Study the following concordance lines.

    a) Some guys **go out** and drink after work.
    b) Many parents are **going out** and buying new laptop computers.
    c) He told me I should **go out** and get myself a new car.
    d) Candidates have to **go out** and raise a lot of money.
    e) We have to **go out** and play as a team.
    f) We had to **go out** and look at new carpets.
    g) I'll just **go out** and buy it, if I find something I really like.

    1. What conjunction often follows the phrasal verb *go out*?
    2. What kind of information follows the conjunction?
    3. How can you summarize the pattern that you have just observed?

4. Using the pattern illustrated above, complete these sentences using your own words and an appropriate form of *go out*:

    a) Last night, I

    ....

    b) Today I plan to

    ....

    c) Some people enjoy

    ....

B.

1. Read the following sentences with *go out of one's way*:

    a) The boss went out of his way to thank everyone personally.

    b) The president has gone out of his way to maintain good relations with the prime minister.

    c) The committee members went out of their way to insist that an agreement could still be reached.

    d) They have made a special effort and gone out of their way to meet everyone.

2. List the verbs that collocate with *go out of one's way*.

3. Does *go out of one's way* appear to have a positive or negative connotation?

4. Explain the meaning of the following use of *go out*. Use a dictionary, if necessary:

My heart goes out to the family of the missing child.

C. Complete the sentences with a suitable form of *go out* (e.g., *is going out*) and one of the words from the box. Be sure to use the correct article (e.g. a/the) with the noun where required:

dark	way	letter	praise	cameras	flirted

1. Last Sunday, the minister .... of his way to .... his staff.
2. The president has .... of his .... to maintain good relations with the prime minister.
3. We .... a lot in high school, but we never really .... together until last year.
4. I pulled myself together and .... to face ....
5. I never .... after ....anymore.
6. I should have been more responsible and read .... before it ....

I think I'd like to go out with Donald Trump

48

Unit 22: KNOW ABOUT something/someone

STUDY THESE SENTENCES

OTHER PATTERNS know (quantity) about
The book covers everything you want to know   1   be aware of, have knowledge of
 about a wedding.   something

EXERCISES

A. Draw a line between the two halves of each sentence.

a. What do high school students know   about the selection process.
b. The more we know   about you, but I get busier and
                                                busier.
c. Parents have a right to know   about finance?
d. He does things nobody knows   about each other, the better.
e. I don't know   about.

B. Study the following concordance lines.

a. I **knew** nothing **about** antiques.
b. Do you **know** anything **about** that topic?
c. We **know** so little **about** climate change.
d. She **knows** a lot **about** making clothes.
e. I'd love to **know** more **about** it.

1. What information occurs between *know* and *about*?

2. Summarize the basic pattern observed above, then write your own sentence
   based on the same pattern.

C. Discussion Question

1. What subject do you know a lot about? How did you learn about it?

2. What subject do you know nothing about? Where could you find out more?

Unit 23: GO AHEAD (with)

STUDY THESE SENTENCES

abc ●

I told them to **go ahead** and start the party without me.	1	carry on, start

IDIOMS

A: Can I ask another question? B: Go ahead, Gail	2	go ahead =an invitation to speak

EXERCISES

A. Study the following concordance lines.

    a. I tried to persuade them not to **go ahead** with the merger
    b. I **went ahead** with it because I didn't want to disappoint my parents
    c. We are planning to **go ahead** with the sale
    d. The mayor will determine whether to **go ahead** with plans to build a new stadium
    e. Is he still planning to **go ahead** with his trip?

    1. What preposition follows the phrasal verb *go ahead*?
    2. What kind of information follows the preposition? Make a list.
    3. How can you summarize the pattern that you have just observed?

B. Complete the sentences with a suitable form of *go ahead* (e.g., *is going ahead*) and one of the words from the box. Be sure to use the correct article (e.g. a/the) with the noun where required:

lunch	plans	insisted	say	agreement

1. Bill, why don't you .... with what you wanted to ....?
2. After months of discussions we finally .... with our ....
3. We have .... to .... with the sale.
4. The company .... on ....
    with its plans.
5. It is 12:30, so maybe we should .... and break
    for ....

50

Unit 24: MEET WITH someone/something

STUDY THESE SENTENCES

Last week the president **met with** three foreign diplomats.

1   **meet** (for business or discussions)

The mayor is hopeful that the new policies will **meet with** public approval.

2   =a focus on the reactions to or consequences of something

EXERCISES

A. **For each sentence decide if** *meet with* **refers to (1)** *meeting as a result of planning* **or (2)** *reactions or consequences* **and write the number on the line.**

1. The company's proposal met with harsh criticism. _____
2. When you have gathered all the information, you are ready to meet with your boss. _____
3. His efforts met with only limited success. _____
4. The peace offering has been met with renewed violence. _____
5. The new bylaws did not meet with public approval. _____
6. The proposed bills met with major skepticism from some Republicans. _____
7. Attempts to introduce a set of revised rules met with vigorous opposition. _____
8. The manager met with the coaches to discuss the problem. _____
9. His claims were met with utter disbelief. _____
10. Talk of the merger was met with cautious optimism. _____

B. **Using the sentences from A, identify all of the collocations relating to** *negative* **reactions about something. The first has been done for you:**

Noun	Collocates with	Example
criticism	harsh	*The company's proposal met with harsh criticism.*

D. **Discussion Question**

1. Have you ever met with a career guidance counselor?

Unit 25: REVIEW
GO OUT, KNOW ABOUT, GO AHEAD, MEET WITH

A. **Using complete sentences, answer these questions about the phrasal verbs examined in units 21-24:**

1. If Lindsey is going out with Ryan, does this mean they are dating?
2. Kayla was aware of the return policy before she bought the DVD player. Does this mean she knew about the policy before buying it?
3. The mayor decides not to go ahead with the plan. Does this mean that he is going to proceed with the plan?
4. The university's admission letters went out on April 1st. Were the letters sent?
5. The client's proposal was met with disapproval. Was the proposal well received?

B. **Read the following statements and decide which people are experiencing negative feelings and which are experiencing positive feelings:**

1. Ann: "Her parents made a special effort at the wedding and went out of their way to meet everyone."
2. Caleb: "You don't know anything about me!"
3. Michelle: "I tried to tell them not to go ahead with it, but they wouldn't listen."
4. Alex: "He knows so much stuff about computers."
5. Chris: "I didn't want to do it, but I went ahead with it anyway."

C. **Replace the underlined word or phrase with the appropriate phrasal verb or idiomatic phrase:**

1. We are planning to proceed with the merger.
2. He is aware of the dangers of skydiving.
3. During the recession, many owners of small companies could no longer operate their businesses.
4. They dated for years before he finally proposed marriage.
5. The check was mailed a week ago.

D. **Correct the errors in these sentences. There is one error in each sentence.**

1. The president has went out of his way to maintain good relations with the United Nations.
2. Is she still planning to going ahead with her trip?
3. We so little know about earthquakes.
4. Last week the teacher meets with three new students.
5. Many parents are going out and buy new laptops for their kids.

Unit 26: COME IN

STUDY THESE SENTENCES

abc ●●●

We need to prevent drugs from **coming in** at the border.	1	enter
As the evidence **comes in**, we can build up a better case.	2	arrive
He **came in** as the new head of department.	3	join an organization/situation
He was disappointed to **come in** second place.	4	=finish a race etc. in first/last/... position

IDIOMS

The umbrella will **come in handy** if it rains.	5	come in handy; come in useful =be useful
The plans have **come in for** a lot of criticism..	6	come in for criticism/blame/ abuse =be criticized/blamed/ abused, etc.

EXERCISES

A. Using the information above, decide which use of *come in* is illustrated in each of the following examples:

1. Gunnison airport only had two planes come in that day. _____
2. Some calls came in from places like Hungary. _____
3. The athlete had high expectations coming in because he plays well here. _____
4. Bill shouted for her to come in. _____
5. The Spanish motorcyclist came in second last year. _____

B. Complete the sentences with a suitable form of *come in* (e.g., *is coming in*) and an appropriate word from the box.

basic	criticism	overwhelming	checks	management

1. The country has .... for intense international ....
2. I have students .... who don't know the .... concepts.
3. Results .... showed an .... victory for the politician.
4. A .... team .... with a new plan during the last quarter.

5. We are waiting for the .... to ....

C. Draw a line between the two halves of each sentence.

1. The US unemployment rate came   in handy today.
2. The new models are coming   in to practice a lot more.
3. Your umbrella will come   in through the walls
4. The coach is getting me to come   in at 6%.
5. Sometimes water comes   in any day now.

D. Discussion Question

What item(s) would come in handy for the following situations?

(a) You are lost in a new city.

(b) You have a headache.

(c) You want to listen to music, but don't want to disturb anybody.

(d) It's cold and snowy outside.

Unit 27: PUT ON something; PUT something ON

STUDY THESE SENTENCES

abc

OTHER PATTERNS put someone on		
I **put** a couple of handouts **on** the table.	1	place something on a concrete object
We want to be able to **put** the test **on** the web.	2	place something on an abstract object
She quickly **put on** her coat and ran out the door.	3	put clothes on your body/add makeup to the face
The school is always **putting on** plays and concerts.	4	put on a show/play

IDIOMS		
I must have **put on** a couple of pounds over Thanksgiving.	5	**put on weight; gain weight** =get heavier by adding fat or muscle
*You're not **putting us on**, are you?*	6	**put somebody on** = joke, or mislead someone
He **put** his career **on hold** and headed to Alaska.	7	**put something/someone on hold** =postpone something for a time
Can I put you on hold?		=wait on the telephone

EXERCISES

A. For each sentence below, decide if *put on* refers to (1) *putting something on a concrete object* or (2) *putting something on an abstract object* and write the number on the line.

1. How many candles do you put on the birthday cake? _____
2. They were put on a flight back to Malaysia. _____
3. Italians put about $700 million on their credit cards each year. _____
4. I couldn't resist the treats they put on the table. _____
5. The company would be put on the auction block in an effort to raise money.

_____

B. Complete the sentences with the correct form of the verb *put* and the particle *on*. If there is one blank space, write the verb form together with the particle in that space. The first one is done for you.

1. Plans to start the new project will be <u>put on</u> (put) hold until the New Year.
2. The government is .... (put) pressure ....
   the university system to increase enrollments.

3. Italians .... (put) about $700 million ....
   their credit cards each year.
4. The school is always .... (put) plays and concerts.
5. A local law .... (put) limits .... rents
   for poor people.

Can you put it on my credit card?

C. Look up *put on* in your dictionary. Note some of the collocations and then add them to
   the appropriate list:

put on X   put X on
_____   _____
_____   _____

Unit 28: MOVE ON

STUDY THESE SENTENCES

abc

OTHER PATTERNS move on to, move ahead on

The delegation arrives in New York tonight and will **move on** to Washington tomorrow.	1	change location
The victim says he is ready to forgive and **move on**.	2	go to the next stage (in life) change to something better
He is **moving on** to his next real estate deal.	3	go to the next stage (in a career/business/sport)
Let's **move on** to item 3 on the agenda.	4	go to the next stage/item (in a meeting)

IDIOMS

The officials said they **moved on** the plan as quickly as they could.	5	**move on** something =carry out/execute something
He welcomed the government's decision to **move ahead on** food aid.	6	**move ahead on** =make progress with something

EXERCISES

A. Using the information above, decide which use of *move on* is illustrated in each of the following examples. Write the number on the line:

1. The four winners move on to the semifinals in May. _____
2. About half the population in this region have moved on in search of jobs. _____
3. Hopefully, the problems are over. I'm going to try to move on. _____
4. Any comments? If not, we can move on. _____
5. Americans need to get this behind them and move ahead on things that are really important. _____
6. The government was slow to move on the oil-for-food program. _____

B. Read each sentences and then answer the question.

1. The group arrives in Los Angeles this afternoon and will move on to Honolulu tomorrow.

   Where will the group be before they travel to Honolulu?

2. He worked for a small legal practice for five years before moving on to greener fields.

Where did the man used to work? Explain what it means to *move on to greener fields*? Use a dictionary, if necessary.

3. She was promoted to assistant editor and later moved on to the post of deputy editor of the Herald.

   How many times has the woman been promoted? What is her current position?

4. About fifty percent of the population in the area has moved on in search of employment.

   Why have so many people left the area?

C. Complete the sentences with a suitable form of *move on* (e.g., *is moving on*) and one of the words from the box. Be sure to use the correct article (e.g. a/the) with the noun where required:

officials	comments	book	foreign	time

1. Seinfeld said no, it's .... to ...., do other things.

2. Any ....? If not, we can ....

3. .... said they .... the plan as quickly as they could.

4. She is .... to her next .... signing next week.

5. Reports say Barcelona's other .... athletes might be ....

D. Discussion Question

   When traveling, do you prefer to stay in one place for a long time or do you prefer to move on to a new place every few days?

Unit 29: GET BACK

STUDY THESE SENTENCES

abc

PATTERNS get back to somewhere/something/someone, get something/someone back, get back at

I went for a walk and **got back** to the hotel at 5 p.m.	1	return
You will **get** your money **back**.	2	have something/someone again
My sleep schedule is **getting back** to normal.	3	return to an abstract place/activity

IDIOMS

They're trying to **get back at Susan**.	4	**get back at** = take revenge
He said he would **get back to me** in a day or so.	5	**get back to someone** =contact somebody at a later date) **get in touch with**
I want to **get back on track** and start exercising again.	6	**get back on track** =return to a previous state, usually for the better

EXERCISES

A. **Study the following concordance lines. Group those which have a similar meaning and rewrite them under the appropriate heading. There are two correct choices for each heading.**

(a) He got back on his bicycle and pedaled home.
(b) The policeman told me I would probably get my bag back, minus the cash.
(c) The banking system may take time getting back on its feet.
(d) The tornado caused a lot of damage, but things are now getting back to normal.
(e) He will return from vacation and get back to work.
(f) It's good to see your career is getting back on track.
(g) The football coach got his job back.
(h) He wanted to get back to the office as soon as possible.
(i) Let's get back to business.

return to/get back to a place

59

get/have something/someone back

return to/get back to/get something back to an abstract   place/activity

return to a previous state, usually for the better

B. Complete the sentences with the correct form of *get* and the particle *back*. If there is one blank space, write the verb form together with the particle in that space.

1. We sent him numerous letters, but he never .... (get) to us.
2. The important thing is to .... (get) the company .... to profitability.
3. I will raise that concern with her and make sure she .... (get) to you.
4. Boeing is trying to .... (get) its production lines .... to normal.
5. After a series of production problems, the factory is .... (get) on track.

C. Rewrite the sentences below by replacing the underlined words in each sentence with an appropriate use of *get back*. Make other adjustments to the sentence where necessary, so that it makes sense.

1. I don't have an answer, so let me <u>call you later.</u>

2. I asked her to call me when she <u>comes in.</u>

3. He was anxious <u>to become involved in the hair care business once again.</u>

4. He is doing it <u>to take revenge on them.</u>

5. That <u>returns</u> to the point Steve brought up.

D. Discussion Question

1. Your friend is depressed because s/he recently lost his/her job. How could you help your friend get back on the right track?

Unit 30: REVIEW
COME IN, PUT ON, MOVE ON, GET BACK

A. Complete the sentences with the correct form of the verb in parentheses and one of the following particles (*in, on, back*). If there is one blank space, write both the verb and particle in the space:

1. We need to prevent drugs from .... (come) at the border.
2. I .... (put) a couple of handouts .... the table.
3. The driver paid for the gas and .... (get) in his truck.
4. The president said we have to .... (move) auto parts and autos.
5. We should .... (put) a lot more emphasis .... literacy skills.

B. Answer yes/no these questions about the phrasal verbs examined in units 26-29:

1. If the new coat you bought is not waterproof, will it come in handy when it rains?

2. If you are sitting in a meeting and the chairperson says, "*Okay, let's move on*", does this mean s/he wants to begin discussing a different subject?

3. If the plumber was able to put his finger on the problem, does he understand what the problem is?

4. If the company's plans have come in for a lot of criticism by the shareholders, does this mean that the shareholders are pleased with the plans?

5. If a house was put on the market this week, does this mean the owners are trying to sell it?

C. Correct the errors in these sentences. There is one error in each sentence.

1. In January there wasn't much money coming on.

2. It is difficult to put on a dollar value the merger.

3. We called him several times, but he never got back at us.

4. The finance ministry is trying to get back the economy on track.

5. Putting your answers on the board.

61

D. Fill in the blanks to complete the word puzzle. In some cases, you will need a verb plus particle:

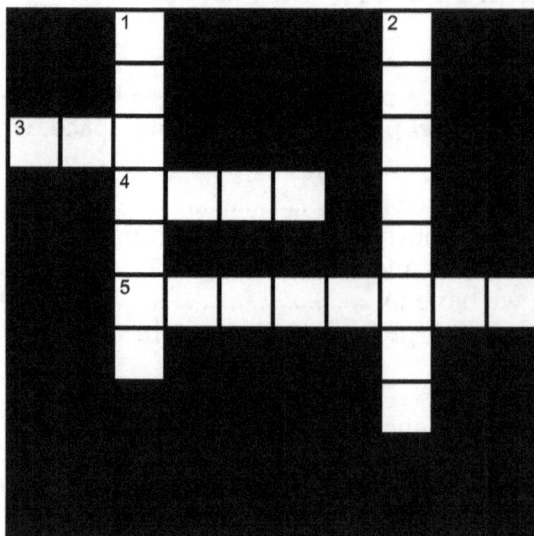

Across

3. The flight was full and so we had to _____ our name on a waiting list.
4. His goal is to get America ____ to the moon.
5. Meteorologists say that there is a lot of information _____ that we still don't fully understand.

Down

1. Once he _____ on schedule, everything was fine.
2. Sylvia worked there for fifteen years before _____ to greener pastures.

Unit 31: GET OUT of something; GET something OUT

STUDY THESE SENTENCES

abc

OTHER PATTERNS get out of (doing) something

He **got out** of the car and walked to the stadium.	1	leave a building or place or situation
Do you think you can **get out** all the Americans who need to be evacuated?	2	remove someone/something from a place/situation
Can you **get** your dictionary **out**?	3	remove from a bag etc. *similar to take out*

IDIOMS

I can't believe that you're trying to **get out of** finishing that job.	4	**get out of doing** something = avoid doing something
The party was **getting** a little **out of hand**.	5	**get out of hand/get out of control** =become too difficult to control
We had to run to **get out of the way** of a speeding car.	6	**get out of the way** =avoid something

EXERCISES

A. Using the information above, decide which use of *get out* is illustrated in each of the following examples. Write the number on the line:

1. I can't believe that you're trying to get out of doing that job. _____
2. The objective is to get the heavy weapons out of the area. _____
3. Let's get out of here. _____
4. It is amazing how quickly a situation can get out of hand. _____
5. People that failed to get out immediately inhaled the hot air. _____

B. Complete the sentences with the correct form of *get out*. If there are two blank spaces, put the particle in the second space.

1. There are fears that the epidemic is .... of control.

2. I had to .... my suit .... for the wedding.

3. Something must be done about the trash before it .... of hand.

4. The Fire Department brought in 300-gallon water tanks for stopping grassfires before they .... of control.

5. The board wants to .... results .... faster.

63

C. Study the collocation patterns below then add to the lists:

(a) get out of X (noun)

-a car
_____
_____
_____

(b) X (noun) got out of hand/got out of control

- the party
_____
_____
_____

(c) get (noun) out of (noun)
-a pen out of my pocket
_____
_____
_____

(d) get out of X (verb + noun)
-doing my homework
_____
_____
_____

D. Investigate the uses of *get out* illustrated in the following examples. Use a dictionary to help you, if necessary.

1. I thought I should come and **get you out of hot water**.

2. He needs to **get his head out of the clouds** and get his feet on the ground.

3. I hope we can **get** something positive **out** of the meeting.

Unit 32: END UP somewhere

STUDY THESE SENTENCES

abc ●●●● ●●●●
●●●

OTHER PATTERNS end up doing something
His family fled the country and **ended up** in
  the US.
I ended up working as a dishwasher.

1 come to be in a place or
   situation

EXERCISES

A. Study the following concordance lines, then answer the questions below:

I don't want my son to **end up** in jail.
The city government may **end up** with a surplus of unspent money.
If we are not careful, we may **end up** in a court of law.
We don't want to **end up** with an unworkable solution.
The money **ended up** in the bank account of the senator.

1. Which prepositions follow the phrasal verb *end up*?

2. What kind of information follows the preposition? Make a list.

3. Following the pattern that you have just observed, write a sentence using your
   own words.

B. Study the following concordance lines, then answer the questions below:

I **ended up** learning a lot while working at the company.
He moved to Manhattan and finally **ended up** working in Los Angeles.
I know you **end up** paying much more than its worth.
The film **ended up** costing $5 million to make.
You could **end up** losing a lot of money unless you pay attention to the details.

1. What kind of information immediately follows the phrasal verb *end up*? Make a list.

2. Following the pattern that you have just observed, write a sentence using your own
   words.

65

C. Complete the sentences with a suitable form of *end up* (e.g., *ended up*) and one of the words from the box. Be sure to use the correct article (e.g. a/the) with the noun where required:

scheme	entire	drunk	surplus	needing	moved

1. He .... five stitches to treat a cut on his arm.

2. He got .... with some friends and .... home with no memory of the evening.

3. He .... to Manhattan and finally .... working in Los Angeles.

4. The city government may .... with .... of unspent money.

5. .... scheme may .... costing as much as $20 billion.

I wonder where I'll end up this time.

Unit 33: PICK UP something; PICK something up

STUDY THESE SENTENCES

OTHER PATTERNS pick up someone, pick someone up

I **picked** my tools **up** and started to work.	1	**lift something** (concrete object)
People often **pick up** colds and other illnesses at work.	2	**get something** (unexpectedly) (abstract object)
The economy is expected to **pick up** again next year.	3	**improve**
Save your work often so that if the computer crashes, you can **pick up** where you left off.	4	**resume**

IDIOMS

The actor used his celebrity status to **pick up** women.	5	**pick up someone** =meet for the purpose of starting a casual relationship

EXERCISES

A. For each sentence below, decide if *pick up* refers to (1) *picking up a concrete object* or (2) *picking up an abstract object* and write the number on the line.

1. The rate at which patients pick up infections in hospitals rose by 5% last year.

2. "We have your bag," he said. "You can pick it up at the office." _____
3. You will need to have a car to pick the children up from school. _____
4. Kids are picking up their new language very quickly. _____
5. Could you pick up the dry-cleaning from Ocean Breeze? _____

B. These sentences illustrate some of the collocations for *pick up*. Draw a line between the two halves of each sentence.

1. The fishing boat picked up	the game's pace.
2. He picked up	steam.
3. The Bulldogs tried to pick up	the SOS signal.
4. He picked up some sort of	the pieces.
5. The online gambling industry is picking up	the tab for the meal.
6. After a bankruptcy someone has to pick up	bug in India.

I'm going to wait until the economy picks up

C. Rewrite the sentences by replacing the underlined word or phrase with the correct form of *pick up* (e.g. *is picking up*).

1. The government may <u>pay for</u> some of the health costs of early retirees.

2. Students need to <u>collect</u> their room keys between 10 a.m. and 5 p.m.

3. His work includes operating an ambulance service that <u>takes</u> many of the wounded.

4. Luckily, sales <u>improved</u> later in the season.

5. Last Friday, a 24-year-old man was <u>arrested</u> at his home and taken into custody.

Unit 34: GIVE UP (doing) something

STUDY THE EXAMPLES

We haven't **given up**, but it will be hard to win the competition.	1	surrender, admit you cannot do something (similar to *give in*)
He is trying to **give up** smoking.	2	stop having, using, or doing something
He **gave up** his American citizenship and went back to India.		

EXERCISES

A. Read these concordance lines, then answer the following questions.

(a) He's **given up** hope of marriage and children
(b) He decided to **give up** drinking
(c) The protesters said they would not **give up** their fight
(d) He was forced to **give up** his job
(e) The woman helped persuade her boyfriend to **give up** two hostages
(f) For many years he refused to **give up** his typewriter for a computer

1. What words are associated with *give up*? Compile a list.

2. The verbs that come before *give up* tell us something interesting about its meaning. What conclusions can you draw about the act of *giving up something* by looking at the preceding verbs?

B. Create full sentences with an appropriate form of *give up* using the words provided in the brackets. The first one has been done for you.

1. (career in politics / spend more time with his family)

   He gave up a career in politics to spend more time with his family   .

2. (photography / join the army)

   ....

3. (her free time / help new immigrants)

   ....

4. (millions of Americans / cigarettes)

....

5. (the baby / adoption)

....

C. Discussion Questions

1. Did you ever give up an activity (e.g. piano lessons) and wished you hadn't?

2. 'If at first you don't succeed, try, try again'. What does this motto mean? How could you offer the same advice using 'give up'?

I'm trying to give up smoking

Unit 35: REVIEW
END UP, GET OUT, PICK UP, GIVE UP

A. Fill in the blanks using the correct form of the verb in brackets. If there is one blank space in the sentence, write the verb and particle there; if there are two blank spaces, write the correct form of the verb in the first space and the particle in the second one.

1. The sun has gone and the wind .... (pick) up.
2. I've .... (give) watching TV during the day.
3. We need to make sure that the information .... (get) to the students on campus.
4. The businessman .... (pick) the phone and pretended to be working on a big deal.
5. If we are not careful, we may .... (end) in a court of law.
6. We dropped Sam and Pat off at 8 a.m. and .... (pick) them .... at 4 p.m.
7. Everyone had .... (give) him .... for dead, but he was found alive and well.
8. It's been too difficult to .... (get) the wounded .... of Grozny sooner.

B. Answer yes or no to the following questions.

1. If you've given up cigarettes, do you still smoke?
2. If a person loves picking up babies, does s/he like holding babies?
3. If a person got of his/her contract and changed jobs, did s/he successfully avoid the contract?
4. If she refused to give up, did she surrender?
5. If a person ends up in hospital, was it expected?
6. The online gambling industry is picking up steam. Is it gaining popularity?

C. Correct the errors in these sentences. There is one error in each sentence.

1. I've cut down on coffee, but I don't think I can give up completely.
2. The company decided to gets out of the computer business.
3. When I went to picked up the car, I found the car rental company had no record of my reservation.
4. I don't want my son ends up in jail.
5. "We'll never given up," he said.
6. The problems have to be solved before they getting out of hand.

Unit 36: DEPEND ON someone/something

STUDY THE EXAMPLES

abc

I **depend on** Alan for his sound advice.	1	rely on or trust someone
The company **depends on** Asia for 40% of its sales.	2	rely on something
Prices vary, **depending on** the model.	3	relating outcome/results to factors or a situation

EXERCISES

A. Using the information above, decide which meaning of *depend on* is illustrated in each of the following examples. Write the number on the line:

1. Mexico's future growth depends heavily on the US economy. _____
2. The price of oil depends upon a multitude of factors. _____
3. There are people depending on me and I don't want to let them down.

   _____
4. Rooms are $95 to $150 depending upon demand. _____
5. Car companies depend heavily on foreign sales. _____

B. Draw a line between the two halves of each sentence.

1. Depending on the type of hotel,	on your perspective.
2. We've been depending too much	on tourism for their livelihood.
3. You can use a hot curry powder or mild,	costs range from $50 - $250.
4. Residents of the Cayman Islands depend	on Susan.
5. What you make of the new information depends	depending on your taste.

C. Complete the sentences with a suitable form of *depending on* (e.g., *is depending on*) and the best choice of words from the box. Be sure to use the correct article (e.g. a/the) with the noun where required:

nutrition	farming	government	rates	it

1. What happens next .... entirely on ....
2. Many consumers .... food labels for .... information.
3. Italy .... for 3% of its gross domestic product.
4. Mortgage .... vary greatly .... the product.
5. .... on what you want.

Unit 37: POINT OUT someone/something

STUDY THE EXAMPLES

abc

OTHER PATTERNS point something/someone out

He **pointed out** a footpath running across the field.	1	physically identify someone/something
The woman **pointed** him **out** to a police sergeant.		
I just want to **point out** that I attended all the lectures.	2	draw attention to something

EXERCISES

A. Study the following concordance lines, then answer the questions below:

(a) The old woman proudly **pointed out** the dried flowers she had prepared.

(b) I could still **point out** the tree we climbed as kids.

(c) He **pointed out** sites to his guests and chatted with vacationers at the mountain resort.

(d) A television viewer called the tournament and **pointed out** the player's violation.

1. What kind of information immediately follows the phrasal verb *point out*? Make a list.

2. Following the pattern that you have just observed, write a sentence using your own words.

B. Study the following concordance lines, then answer the questions below:

(a) He **pointed out** that the Ancient Greeks had no word for race.

(b) They **point out** that NATO does not produce its own intelligence

(c) The ski industry is quick to **point out** that bicycling is more dangerous than skiing

(d) He **points out** that Cuba continues to hold hundreds of political prisoners

1. What kind information immediately follows the phrasal verb *point out*?

2. Following the pattern that you have just observed, write a sentence using your own words.

C. Discussion Question:

In what kind of situation might somebody point out interesting landmarks? grammar mistakes? a celebrity? Use your imagination.

Unit 38: WORK OUT something

STUDY THE EXAMPLES

abc

OTHER PATTERNS work something out, work out

The amount **works out** to be $4.26 per share.	1	**calculate** similar to *come to*
I'll try to **work** something **out**. The Security Council is expected to **work out** details of the new procedures.	2	**understand** similar to *find a solution/solve a problem*
We're hoping that this is really going to **work out** well. I had imagined a peaceful few days. It didn't **work out**.	3	**lead to a good result/outcome**

IDIOMS

He **works out** at a small local gym..	4	**work out** =do physical exercise

EXERCISES

A. Using the information above, decide which use of *work out* is illustrated in each of the following examples. Write the number on the line:

1. He knew all along that things would work out for the best.   _____

2. He began working out 5 days a week.   _____

3. Some new arrangement is sure to be worked out.   _____

4. The French liquor company said that the loss works out to 9.8 euros a share.

        _____

B. Read the following concordance lines. Which nouns appear to collocate with *work out*? Fill in the blanks below with your answers. The first one has been done for you:

The government is hoping to **work out** an agreement
The committee will **work out** a proposal
He knew all along that things would **work out** for the best.
Some new arrangement is sure to be **worked out**
Some details still have to be **worked out**
I am sure that a compromise can be **worked out**

<u>**work out** something</u>
- <u>an agreement</u>

- _____

- _____

- _____

- _____

- _____

I hope this works out

Unit 39: GO WITH someone/something

STUDY THE EXAMPLES

The bodyguard **went with** him everywhere.   **1**   accompany
The silk tie **goes** perfectly **with** that outfit.   **2**   match
If I want style, I'll probably **go with** a sports   **3**   choose
 car.

EXERCISES

A. Using the information above, decide which use of *go with* is illustrated in each of the following examples. Write the number on the line:

1. He bought me a painting he thought would go splendidly with my apartment. _____

2. We decided to go with a larger firm. _____
3. I used to go to church with my parents. _____

B. Rewrite the sentences by replacing the underlined word or phrase with the correct form of *go with*:

1. She bought me a purse that <u>matches</u> perfectly with my shoes.

2. The safest option is to <u>choose</u> what is popular.

3. People want to leave to escape urban crime and the fear that <u>is associated with it</u>.

4. I asked if I could <u>accompany</u> them to the shops.

5. His dog <u>followed</u> him everywhere.

C. Complete the sentences with a suitable form of *go with* (e.g., *is going with*) and one of the words from the box. Be sure to use the correct article (e.g. a/the) with the noun where required:

personnel	who	convinced	rates and services	dots	feeling

1. Once he became .... of the plan, he ....
   it 100 percent.

2. You have to do what you think is right; you have to .... your
   gut ....

3. Stripes just don't ....

4. Do we make any .... changes or .... what we have?

5. We'll .... the company that offers better ....

6. If you don't know your way around, ... someone
.... does.

Does this bowtie go with my jacket?

D. Discussion Question

1. What does it mean to 'go with your gut (feeling)'? Explain using your own words. Use a dictionary, if necessary.

2. Read the following statement:

There is some disagreement about whether economic growth goes hand in hand with democracy.

In your own words, explain the expression 'go hand in hand with'. Use a dictionary, if necessary. Try to think of other examples.

Unit 40: REVIEW
DEPEND ON, POINT OUT, WORK OUT, GO WITH

A. Complete the sentences with an appropriate form of the verb in parentheses and one of the following particles (on, out, with). If there is one blank space in the sentence, write the verb and particle there; if there are two blank spaces, write the correct form of the verb in the first space and the particle in the second one:

1. Fitzpatrick, who .... (go) to the United Nations School .... him, became a government informant in 1978.
2. Smaller islands that .... (depend) banana exports could be hurt by NAFTA.
3. Frank .... (point) his tattoos while speaking about his involvement in a gang.
4. The longer hours and new check-in system have allowed more people to .... (work) comfortably in the Rec center.
5. .... (depend) our initial assumptions, we all come to many different conclusions.

B. Choose the best answer to fill in the blanks:

1. They are expected to work out differences. This means____:
   (a) they will probably solve their problem
   (b) they will probably not solve their problem
   (c) they are going to work out at different times

2. Your co-worker picks you up on time to drive to work every morning. This means____:
   (a) s/he is unreliable
   (b) s/he is not punctual
   (c) you can depend on him/her

3. The teacher pointed out the mistake to his students. This means ____:
   (a) the teacher identified the mistake to his students
   (b) the teacher gave the students points for their mistake
   (c) the teacher made a point

4. While shopping, a customer has a difficult time deciding between two sweaters. She finally decides to go with the red. This means____:
   (a) she chose a blue sweater
   (b) she bought a red sweater
   (c) she did not buy anything

5. Lori works out a lot. This means ____:
    (a) she does not have an office
    (b) she exercises regularly
    (c) she is a good problem solver

C. Correct the errors in these sentences. There is one error in each sentence.

1. When they went, I just couldn't went with them.

2. Depending with the radio station, station management and even DJs are paid at some stations.

3. He could look to his allies to form a government or going with a non-partisan figure

4. I needed time to myself to work what I wanted to do.

5. He guides visitors through the zoo, points out where the animals are housed.

D. Read the following sentences and then answer the questions about them:

1. There would be a television at each piece of equipment so that people could surf channels while they are working out.
   What activity can people do while they are exercising?

2. The car company will provide engines, transmissions, and other key parts and technologies and depend on local suppliers for other parts.
   Who will the company rely on for some of its parts?

3. This year our company went with agencies we had long-standing relationships with.
   Why did the company choose the agencies?

4. We will look at the United States' main wolf populations and the controversy that often accompanies them.
   According to this, what often goes with the wolf populations?

5. The defense attorney pointed out that his client had never before been convicted of a crime.
   In this case, the attorney drew attention to what fact about his client?

Unit 41: TAKE ON something/someone

STUDY THE EXAMPLES

abc

OTHER PATTERNS take something/someone on

In my new job I will have to **take on** additional responsibilities.	1	carry/accept a job/responsibility
The producer **took** him **on** as an assistant director.	2	employ someone
Some musicals have **taken on** the characteristics of pop music.	3	adopt, develop an appearance/quality
Some new start-up companies are ready to **take on** the traditional telephone companies..	4	compete with

IDIOMS

The plan has **taken on a life of its own**.	5	take on a life of its own =develop independently or unpredictably

EXERCISES

A. Using the information above, decide which use of *take on* is illustrated in each of the following examples. Write the number on the line:

1. A new version of "Romeo and Juliet" takes on a MTV flavor. _____
2. The legal assistants took on much of the workload in preparing the case. _____
3. When his company grew in size, he took on a partner. _____
4. Tomorrow the Pistons take on the Spurs. _____

B. Complete the sentences with a suitable form of *take on* (e.g., *is taking on*) and one of the words/phrases from the box. Be sure to use the correct article (e.g. a/the) with the noun where required:

complexity   work   investors   project   negative connotation

1. The word *liberal* has .... in American politics.
2. We are so busy that we cannot .... any more .... right now.
3. When Stevens .... he didn't know how hard it would be.
4. The latest tax laws .... a new level of ....
5. .... too much risk is a common problem for ....

C. **These sentences illustrate some of the collocations for *take on*. Draw a line between the two halves of each sentence.**

1. You can't ask a school to take on   fresh urgency as fears of an epidemic grow.

2. The issue has taken on   the responsibility for students from other districts.

3. He has taken on   the challenge of playing an older woman.

4. The traditional institution has taken on   a new lease of life.
5. The 21-year-old actress agreed to take on   a decidedly modern tone.
6. Each of the countries has taken on   the immigration case.
7. The lawyer agreed to take on   debt for a different reason.

D. **Rewrite the sentences by replacing the underlined word or phrase with the correct form of *take on* (e.g. *is taking on*).**

1. The author <u>was hired by</u> Knopf, a major American publisher.

2. The animal rights campaigner <u>has advocated against</u> some of the biggest US firms.

3. At night, the town <u>assumes</u> a different character.

4. Netscape tried to <u>compete against</u> Microsoft with its web-browser.

5. As managers <u>assume</u> more and more responsibilities, they have less time to encourage and inspire their subordinates.

Unit 42: PUT OUT something; PUT something OUT

STUDY THE EXAMPLES

abc ●

OTHER PATTERNS be put out

The World Health Organization **put out** a report on malaria.	1	release, broadcast
Putting out forest fires can be a very difficult and time-consuming task. (Putting fires out ...)	2	extinguish, stop something from burning
We **put out** the garbage every Tuesday morning. (Put the garbage	3	place outside
The singer **puts out** a lot of recordings, but has stopped playing concerts.	4	produce
I was very **put out** by the disruption caused by the email server going down.	5	be upset/annoyed

IDIOMS

The actress was confident about her performance. "I **put myself out there**. I really worked hard," she said.	6	put oneself out there =take a risk, work hard

EXERCISES

A. Using the information above, decide which use of *put out* is illustrated in each of the following examples. Write the number on the line:

1. The publishing company puts out newspapers in 10 cities. _____
2. I would argue that you ought to pay for the trash you put out. _____
3. The rebel leader put out a tough statement warning about further attacks.

   _____
4. A fire extinguisher was used to put the fire out. _____

B. Study these idiomatic uses of *put out*. Match each sentence (1-4) with its correct definition (a-d) below. Use a dictionary if necessary.

1. The old car resembles a piece of farm equipment <u>put out to pasture</u>.
2. The director said she was tired of "<u>putting out fires</u>" and so she resigned.
3. The horse had broken its leg and we had to <u>put it out of its misery</u>.
4. A collision at the Daytona 500 <u>put</u> two cars <u>out of action</u>.

(a) stop from suffering
(b) disqualify from a job or event
(c) deal with problems in an organization
(d) made to retire/consider unacceptable due to old age

C. Complete the sentences with the correct form of *put out* (e.g. *is putting out*) and one of the words from the box. Be sure to use the correct article (a/the) with the noun where required.). If there are two blank spaces in the sentence, then write both the verb and particle together in one space.

White House	leg	questions	fine	fire extinguisher

1. .... was used to .... (put) the fire ....

2. The runner injured her ...., ... (put) her
    .... of the Games.

3. We'll .... (put) a formal written statement, and then Jennifer will
    take ....

4. The Senator claimed that .... was .... (put)
    misleading information

5. Kickback Records has .... (put) two .... CD Collections.

D. Discussion Questions

1. Which band has put out more albums to date: The Rolling Stones or Madonna?

2. Which company puts out better products: Toshiba or Macintosh?

Unit 43: FOLLOW UP something

STUDY THE EXAMPLES

abc

OTHER PATTERNS follow something up, follow up

A. *The budget will address the health care needs of America's children.*	1	continue a topic
B. *Just to **follow up**; does that include Medicare and Medicaid?*		
The FBI is required to **follow up** any complaints.	2	investigate
In science, it is usual to **follow up** an important finding with more experiments.	3	perform an action in response to a previous action
The government proposed a cut in personal income taxes and **followed that up** with plans to reduce corporate taxes.		

EXERCISES

A. **Study the following concordance lines, then answer the questions below:**

   (a) She plans to follow up the analysis with further studies next year
   (b) Each potential supernova discovery is followed up with additional observations using the Hubble telescope
   (c) The tennis player followed up his Olympic Gold Medal with a victory in Cincinnati.

   1. What preposition often appears after the phrasal verb *follow up*?

   2. What kind of information follows this preposition? Make a list.

   3. Following the pattern that you have just observed, write a sentence using your own words.

B. **Study the following concordance lines, then answer the questions below:**

   (a) The police said they would **follow up** on any leads that came in
   (b) Our analyst, Jane Cook, is happy to **follow up** on any questions that you might have.
   (c) Reporters **followed up** on a story about the official posted on a web site.
   (d) The British police have been **following up** on the kidnapping allegation.
   (e) The kitchen staff takes suggestions and **follows up** on them.

   1. What preposition comes after the phrasal verb *follow up*?

84

2. What kind of information follows this preposition? Make a list.

3. Following the pattern that you have just observed, write a sentence using your own words.

C. Complete the sentences with a suitable form of *follow up* (e.g., *followed up*) and one of the words from the box. Be sure to use the correct article (e.g. a/the) with the noun where required:

consultant	letter	people	wages	chin

1. Police said they are .... on 36 tips received from .... who were in the area at the time of the robbery.
2. The U.S. Ambassador is .... on .... President Clinton sent to Yeltsin.
3. In the ninth, he hit Buenos's .... with a left hook but couldn't ....
4. The CEO .... on a promise made last year and raised .... by 5 percent.
5. .... can help formulate a new plan and then .... to make sure progress is made.

D. Complete these sentences in your own words by demonstrating an appropriate use of *follow up*. The first sentence has been done for you.

1. If you write a letter to complain, <u>follow up with a phone call.</u>

2. If you interview for a new job, ...

3. If you spend the weekend at a friend's condo, ...

4. If you are given a good suggestion, ...

Unit 44: MAKE UP something

STUDY THE EXAMPLES

abc

OTHER PATTERNS make something up

Sales to Japan **make up** 90% of the company's international business.	1	comprise, amount to
We can easily **make up** a multiple-choice test.	2	invent, create (sometimes in order to deceive)
The jury decided the story was a hoax and that he **made** the whole thing **up**.		
McQueen said that town hall has offered to **make up** if he signs a document promising not to speak to the press about the local scandal.	3	become friendly again after a fight
California still hasn't **made up** for jobs lost in the last recession.	4	add enough of something to reach a target
He used to get very angry and shout at people over trivial matters and then try to **make it up** afterward.	5	make it up— do something to show you are sorry, repay a favor

IDIOMS

I **made up my mind** to get back into racing	6	make up my mind =decide
He is fast and is able to **make up ground** in a short time	7	make up ground =do something to compensate for lost speed/distance
Boeing told NASA that it could **make up for lost time**	8	make up for lost time =do something to compensate for lost time

EXERCISES

A. Rewrite the sentences by replacing the underlined word with a suitable form of *make up* (e.g. *is making up*):

1. Oil <u>comprises</u> up to 25 percent of Venezuela's gross domestic product.

2. We don't know how much money we lost because the numbers were <u>fabricated</u>.

3. The Senator said she hadn't <u>decided</u> about running for President.

4. Artificial snow can <u>compensate</u> for a thin snowfall, but it is very expensive.

5. I had to give a telephone number and so I <u>invented</u> one.

B. These sentences illustrate some of the collocations for *make up*. Draw a line between the two halves of each sentence.

1. I managed to make up
2. The governors have until Saturday to make up
3. Boeing told NASA that it could make up

4. The partner made up

5. I made up

an excuse and left the party early.
their minds.

the lost ground and finish the race on top.
a story that I was stealing from the firm.
for lost time on the space project.

C. Study these examples of *make up*, then complete the questions:

Group (A)

Women only **make up** about 12% of the members of Congress
Network services **make up** 45% of the company's revenue
Organic food **makes up** a growing percentage of retail food sales
American troops **make up** about half of a 1,000-man peace-keeping mission

Group (B)

The plan calls for an executive body **made up** of representatives from different regions
The committee is **made up** of doctors and representatives of the local community
The law was approved by the upper house of Parliament, **made up** of representatives of Germany's 16 states
The company appointed a committee **made up** of outside directors to investigate the problem

1. Use the examples from Group (A) to complete this table. The first one has been done for you:

Women	make up	about 12%	of the members of congress

2. Use the examples from Group (B) to complete this table. The first one has been done for you:

an executive body	made up	of	representatives...
the committee			
the upper house of parliament			
a committee			

3. Exercises 1 and 2 illustrate two possible patterns of *make up*. These patterns may be summarized by the following statements:

(i)   noun *makes up* X [amount] of noun
(ii) noun (is) *made up of* noun

Tell which of these patterns matches example Group (A) and which matches example Group (B):

....

4. Following the same patterns that you have just observed, write two new sentences using your own words.

D. Discussion Question

How do you respond to the following statement: "We find that people often make up phony email addresses when completing online forms"?

Unit 45: REVIEW
TAKE ON, PUT OUT, FOLLOW UP, MAKE UP

A. Replace the underlined word or phrase with the appropriate form of *take on, put out, follow up,* or *make up*:

1. The Justice Department <u>released</u> a statement on the case yesterday.
2. When Stevens <u>accepted</u> the project, he didn't know how hard it would be.
3. Women in Iran <u>comprise</u> a third of the workforce and half the university population.
4. The police have been <u>investigating</u> the kidnapping allegation.
5. Many companies are reluctant to <u>hire</u> former drug addicts.
6. Some musicals have <u>adopted</u> the characteristics of pop music.
7. The Senator claimed that the White House was <u>leaking</u> misleading information.
8. I used to <u>compose</u> songs in my head.
9. We don't know how to deal with this issue yet, but let's <u>make it known</u>.
10. It would be like trying to <u>extinguish</u> fires with gasoline.

B. Draw a line between the two halves of each sentence.

1. Who would make up	putting him out of action.
2. The Telegraph is put out	have followed up by investing a further $120 million.
3. Livingston strained a muscle,	be able to make her mind up.
4. Several venture capital firms	by the North American News Company.
5. We believe the customer should	a story like that?

C. Fill in the blanks with the correct form of the appropriate phrasal verb (*take on, put out, follow up,* or *make up*). If there are two blank spaces, write the particle in the second space:

1. The government needs to help the workers .... of jobs in manufacturing.
2. A consultant can help formulate a new plan and then .... to make sure progress is made.
3. I felt that I had let my teammates and fans down, but I am going to .... it .... to them this year.
4. The executive will .... a more powerful role within the company.
5. The inspector failed to .... on complaints made by workers at the factory.

Unit 46: GET AT something/someone

STUDY THE EXAMPLES

abc

They couldn't **get at** the guns because they were kept in a locked cabinet.	1	reach
The aim is to **get at** the truth.	2	uncover/discover/reveal
What are you **getting at**?	3	= *What do you mean?*
Instead of working together, we **got at** each other.	4	criticize, argue

EXERCISES

A. Using the information above, decide which use of *get at* is illustrated in each of the following examples. Write the number on the line:

1. The study aims to get at the reasons for the increased risk of cancer. _____
2. What are you trying to get at? _____
3. The shark tried to get at him through the bars of the cage. _____
4. Instead of getting along, we got at each other's throats. _____

B. Complete the sentences with a suitable form of *get at* (e.g., *is getting at*) and one of the words from the box. Be sure to use the correct article (e.g. a/the) with the noun where required:

poems	section	heart	city workers

1. It is sometimes difficult to .... the meaning of ....

2. .... had to take up the pavement to .... the broken water main.

3. What Gail is .... is really .... of the matter.

4. I may have to open a .... of the wall to .... the cable.

C. Rewrite the following sentences using an appropriate form of *get at*. Make any other necessary adjustments to the sentences so that they make sense:

1. What do you mean?
   ....

2. I don't see what you're trying to say.
   ....

3. I think I know what you mean.
   ....

Unit 47: GET ON something

STUDY THE EXAMPLES

Sometimes I **get on** my bicycle and go someplace alone.	1 mount (a bicycle/horse) get on a bus. train
We want to **get on** TV.	2 appear on (abstract object)
A: *There's a problem with the computer network* B: *I'll **get on** it right away*	3 attend to something, work on something (usually immediately)
Let's have coffee and then we'll **get on** with our work.	4 start or continue doing something
At home I was **getting on** the kids for trivial things all the time.	5 criticize someone

EXERCISES

A. For each sentence below, decide if *get on* refers to (1) *getting on a concrete object* or (2) *getting on an abstract object.* Write the number on the line:

1. Some people will do just about anything to get on television. _____

2. I got on the phone and booked a ticket to Atlanta. _____

3. We had to get on the road to make it home before dark. _____

4. Sean gets on his Harley-Davidson and heads into the mountains. _____

5. The Owls got on the scoreboard first with a field goal. _____

B. Complete the sentences with a suitable form of *get on* (e.g., *is getting on*) and one of the words from the box. Be sure to use the correct article (e.g. a/the) or personal pronoun (e.g. my, his, etc.) with the noun where required:

life	doors	father	it	bicycle

1. Sometimes I .... and go someplace alone.
2. I think Bill is interested in .... with ....
3. Monica .... the plane and flew to California to be with ....
4. Let's .... with ....
5. We .... the train and .... closed immediately.

91

B. Here are some idiomatic uses of *get on*. Match each use of *get on* (sentences 1-4) with its correct definition (a-d) below. Use a dictionary if necessary:

1. As Clare **got on in years**, she noticed how badly the elderly were treated.
2. My mother is always **getting on my case** about my clothes.
3. He said that from his experience, we wouldn't be able to **get on top** of this.
4. I just assumed they were trying to **get on my good side**.
5. Sometimes my coworkers **get on my nerves**.

(a) be in control of something
(b) be irritating
(c) complain or criticize constantly
(d) make someone pleased with your actions
(e) become older

1. _____   2. _____   3. _____   4. _____   5. _____

D. Discussion Question

React to the following statement:

Some people will do just about anything to get on television.

Do you agree or disagree?

Unit 48: BELIEVE IN someone/something

STUDY THE EXAMPLES

Yes, I believe in God. I go to church once a month.

George believes in patience.

The manager believes in his team.

1 **believe in God/ghosts/fairies** = be certain that they exist
2 **believe in something** = support something
3 **believe in someone** = have confidence in them

EXERCISES

A. Using the information above, decide which use of *believe in* is illustrated in each of the following examples. Write the number on the line:

1. I always believed in myself. _____

2. The survey found that 67% of Americans believe in some form of afterlife.
_____

3. We believe in the principles of free trade. _____

B. Create full sentences with an appropriate form of *believe in* using the words provided in the brackets. The first one has been done for you:

1. (George / patience)
   George believes in patience.

2. (Everybody / something)
   ....

3. (We / freedom of choice)
   ....

4. (I / don't / mixing business with pleasure)
   ....

5. (It is important / your chances)
   ....

C. Discussion Question

How would you react to the statement that *Many Americans believe in UFOs*? Do you believe in UFOs?

Unit 49: PUT UP something/someone

STUDY THE EXAMPLES

abc

OTHER PATTERNS put something/someone up, put up with something/someone

She dressed formally and **put** her hair **up**.	1	raise, put in a higher position
We'll **put** you **up** at the hotel of your choice.	2	stay with someone or at a hotel
I was **put up** with this wonderful family, the Taylors.		
The police **put up** barricades to block off the road.	3	put up a building/structure- erect/build/assemble
He **put up** a "Do Not Disturb" sign on his door.	4	put up a sign/poster etc - attach it to a wall, etc

EXERCISES

A. Using the information above, decide which use of *put up* is illustrated in each of the following examples. Write the number on the line:

1. Public money is spent on putting up homeless families in hotels. _____
2. He suddenly put his arm up and we saw the gun. _____
3. We'll put a sign-up sheet up on the board. _____
4. The Red Cross put up a tent near the scene of the accident. _____

B. Here are some idiomatic uses of the phrasal verb *put up*. Draw a line between each use of *put up* (sentences 1-4) and its correct definition. Use a dictionary if necessary.

1. We amateurs are really tired of **putting up a fight**.   tolerate

2. Universal Pictures is **putting up $1.8 million** for the film rights.   offer for sale

3. The Prudential Center was **put up for sale** in November.   oppose or resist

4. I couldn't continue to **put up with** all the fights and arguments.   provide money

C. Discussion Question

In your own words, explain the meaning of the following expression: *It's time to put up or shut up.* Use a dictionary, if necessary.

Unit 50: REVIEW
GET AT, GET ON, BELIEVE IN, PUT UP

A. Answer true or false to the following statements:

1. If you 'put up a fight', you oppose something.
2. If somebody responds to you by asking, 'What are you getting at?' s/he probably needs more information from you.
3. If your uncle has a problem with self-confidence, he believes in himself.
4. If two people are constantly 'getting on each other', they are getting along well.
5. If the teacher tells you to 'get on with your work', s/he wants you to stop doing it.

B. Replace the underlined word or phrase with an appropriate phrasal verb. Make any other necessary adjustments to the sentences so that they make sense:

1. Soldiers were <u>housed</u> in inadequate bases or hotels.

2. Academics are always trying to <u>uncover</u> ideas.

3. What she does <u>support</u> is more power for women.

4. Developers have violated rules in this city in recent years to <u>build</u> high rises.

5. My mother is always <u>criticizing me</u> about my boyfriend.

C. Find the errors. There is one error in each sentence:

1. The city's defenders were putting in stiff resistance.

2. Democrats believes in public education.

3. I suppose we were both so busy get on with our lives.

4. What Gail is gets at is really important.

5. We had to got on with running our companies.

Unit 51: Test your knowledge

A. **Choose the correct particle to complete these sentences:**

1. I'd like to set _____ a meeting with Janice.
   (a) ahead (b) up (c) in (d) through

2. The employees put _____ long hours at the office.
   (a) out (b) in (c) up (d) through

3. I can depend _____ my brother to help me.
   (a) with (b) into (c) back (d) on

4. What we're trying to get _____ is the difference between high and low risk patients.
   (a) in (b) at (c) up (d) out

5. I convinced him to get _____ of the car.
   (a) back (b) out (c) on (d) up

6. Let me go _____ some of the issues that came up yesterday.
   (a) into (b) in (c) ahead (d) through

B. **Complete each sentence the correct form of the verb in brackets and one of the following particles (at, back, on, out, up):**

1. I just .... (get) from the gym.
2. He .... (look) me for a few seconds and didn't say anything.
3. I'm going to be .... (work) this electricity deal.
4. Many of the new products .... (aim) children.
5. After I .... (get) of college, I worked in San Francisco.
6. Our anniversary is .... (come) soon.

C. **Rewrite the sentences by replacing the underlined word with a phrasal verb based on the verb provided in brackets:**

1. It's nice to <u>wear</u> a new dress and a new pair of shoes. (put)
2. I'm not <u>returning</u> to school. (go)
3. He decided to <u>accept</u> the challenge. (take)
4. What's <u>happening</u> in the White House? (go)
5. Maybe you should <u>take</u> the next plane. (get)
6. Let's <u>skip</u> to another question. (move)
7. They couldn't <u>access</u> the guns because they were locked in a cabinet. (get)
8. The workmen <u>installed</u> new doors and windows. (put)
9. I am hoping to <u>start</u> my own company. (set)
10. We <u>finish</u> a box of cereal every two days. (go)

Answer Key

Unit 1: Look at
A. 1. 1 2. 2 3. 4 4. 2 5. 1 6. 3 7. 5
B.
1. The panel will look at both sides of the tax issue.
2. Most people look at it as an investment.
3. The way we look at fashion is about to change.
4. We stopped to look at a car for sale.
5. Let's go to page 2 and look at question number 4.
C.
1. I always look at a problem and try to solve it step by step.
2. If you look at an average family with two kids, they would pay about $400 in taxes.
3. The accountant looked at the sales figures for July.
4. He picked up the gold coin and looked at it carefully.
5. I am always looking at magazines in the bookstore.
6. He often looks at his computer to check for new email.
D. *Students' answers will vary.*
1. He is going to look at it carefully and then make a decision.
2. Maybe you should have a doctor look at it.

Unit 2: Deal with
A. 1
B. 1. 3 2. 1 3. 1 4. 2 5. 1
C.
1. The neighbors are going to have a tough time dealing with those people.
2. There was a recognition that corruption is a problem and that it has to be dealt with.
3. The translators have to deal with thousands of pages of documents.
4. In my field of work, you deal with a wide variety of issues.
D
1. Here are some techniques to deal with unwanted email.
2. With proper planning, you can deal with student loan repayments.
3. The study offers strategies for dealing with stress.
4. People dealing with depression often wish for happier days.
5. You cannot deal with impossible people the same way you deal with everyone else.
E. *Students' answers will vary.*

Unit 3: Do with
A. 1. b, c 2. c, d 3. a, b, d 4. a, c 5. b
B.
1. The defendant said he had nothing to do with the robbery.
2. She said her success had to do with weight training.
3. The film star enjoys relaxing with her husband, who has nothing to do with show business.
4. The army denied that it had anything to do with the attack.
5. The high price of oil has little to do with the drop in share prices.
6. His attitude had a lot to do with his upbringing in Texas.
7. I have a question. It has to do with the overall goal of the report.

Unit 4: Go back
A. 1. 3 2. 2 3. 1 4. 3 5. 1
B. *Students' answers will vary*
If you have to go back to the drawing board, it means that you have to start something again because whatever you were doing before has been unsuccessful. A similar expression is *to go back to square one.*
C. *Students' answers will vary. This is one set of possible answers:*
1. He went back to school to finish his degree.
2. There's no going back to where we were.
3. We could go back and see what she said.
4. Her involvement in the museum goes back 10 years.
5. They just got back from a long trip.
6. The employers and unions will have to go back to the negotiating table
D. *Students' answers will vary.*

Unit 5: REVIEW
A.
1. I'd have to <u>go back</u> and <u>look at</u> the letter.
2. I don't think gender has anything <u>to do with</u> it.
3. Dr. Johnson will lecture on topics <u>dealing with</u> diet and exercise.
4. The politician claimed that he had nothing <u>to do with</u> the decision.
5. We're trying to move the start date. In the interim, we are <u>looking at</u> other options.
B.
1. The government is <u>looking at</u> different strategies for meeting greenhouse gas targets
2. If you can't <u>deal with</u> the heat, get out of the kitchen.
3. The cake's delicious taste <u>has to do with</u> the high quality of chocolate used in the recipe.
4. After she <u>looked at</u> everything that's in the booklet, she still had real concerns.
5. His controversial book <u>deals with</u> the final hours of Princess Diana's life.
6. You are <u>looking at</u> 5 years in prison.
7. He has had a good track record <u>going back</u> several years.
C.
1. negative 2. negative 3. positive 4. negative 5. positive 6. positive 7. negative
D.
1. The mayor has nothing to do <u>with</u> education policy.
2. His criminal record goes back ∅ 10 years.
3. She loves anything to do <u>with</u> cooking.
4. You have to look <u>at</u> a job and decide if it is what you want.
5. Our firm will continue to deal <u>with</u> the Fortune 500 companies.
6. I think we are looking <u>at</u> sometime mid-morning for the meeting.
7. Sara and Jack just got back <u>from</u> their vacation in the Bahamas.
8. The guidelines deal <u>with</u> topics such as health and welfare.

Unit 6: Come up
A. 1. 3 2. 7 3. 6 4. 2 5. 1 6. 2 7. 9 8. 5
B.
1. The government failed to come up with a solution to the country's debt problem.
2. The chip industry is coming up against a brick wall.
3. We should encourage students to guess if they can't come up with an answer.
4. We thought we could win the game, but we came up short.

5. I won't be able to go to the movie; something's come up.

6. The sun comes up around 6 a.m.

C. 1. a 2. b 3. b, c, d 4. a, b, c

D. *Students' answers will vary*

Unit 7: Go on

A. 1. 5 2. 3 3. 1 4. 2 5. 8

B.

1. The younger brother went on to study electronics and worked as an electrician.

2. Last night, the company's spokesperson went on ABC's news program.

3. There is a lively discussion going on between those in favor of the changes and those who oppose the changes.

4. He isn't upset, but that's because he really doesn't know what's going on.

5. What in the world is going on here?

6. We'll add to the list as we go on.

C. *Students' answers will vary.*

1. I'm sure there will be some more meetings as the week goes on.

2. Unfortunately the speeches went on for most of the evening.

3. What is going on at work?

4. The restoration work has gone on for roughly three years now.

D. *Students' answers will vary.*

Unit 8: Come back

A.

1. Store owners are hoping that advertising will encourage shoppers to come back to the mall.   *return*

2. The issue comes back to the point John was making.   *return*

3. It took several hours, but the power finally came back on around noon.   *restart*

4. Then she tried to come back at me with some snide remark. *reply*

5. It's all coming back to me now!   *remember*

B. *Students' answers will vary.*

1. If her words came back to haunt her it means that there were consequences for something that the woman said.

2. If her husband never came back from the war, it's because he was probably killed.

3. If the test came back negative, the patient probably doesn't have diabetes.

4. If Sandy has come back from an injury, she has returned to being healthy and normal again.

C. *Students' answers will vary.*

1. What are your travel plans?

2. That sounds great. You must really be looking forward to it.

3. I'm really hoping to relax a lot on this trip and catch up on some sleep. I need the break.

4. Thanks. Me too.

D. *Students' answers will vary.*

Unit 9: Work on

A.

1. The architect is working on a new design for a skyscraper.

2. The pharmaceutical company has been working on drugs to reduce blood pressure.

3. The singer is working on a new solo album.

4. The psychiatrist suggested he work on improving his self-esteem.

5. Scientists must be immunized before working on dangerous viruses.

6. We had been working on them to change their policy.
7. The chairperson was working on the idea that we'd reach an agreement this week.
B. *Students' answers may vary slightly.*
1. The popular singer is working on a new solo album.
2. The company is working on correcting the problem.
3. A veterinarian works on sick or injured animals.
4. The author is currently working on a novel set in Las Vegas.
5. The mathematician is working on a calculus problem to prove a theory.
6. The teacher is working on his students to do their homework.
7. I'm working on the assumption that a meeting will take place very soon.
C. *Students' answers will vary.*

Unit 10: REVIEW
A.
1. You'll need to be creative in order to come up with some new ideas.
2. I need to rest for a while, but you should go on ahead. I'll catch up.
3. After restarting the computer, Windows XP doesn't come up on the screen.
4. I wonder what would happen if the boat didn't come back to get us.
5. After the semifinals, the team went on to win the championship title.
6. My colleague came up with a proposal for improving our performance.
7. The writer has been working on Reagan's biography for ten years.
8. The American people see what is going on and they don't like it.
B. 1. no 2. yes 3. no 4. no 5. yes 6. no 7. yes 8. no 9. yes 10. yes 11. no 12. no
C.
1. I'll come back to this topic in a minute.
2. We thought we could win the competition, but we came up short.
3. As time goes on, things will get better.
4. He didn't like the dorm, so he went back to live with his grandmother.
5. Our plan didn't work out and so now we have to go back to square one.

Unit 11: Go through
A. 1. 1 2. 4 3. 2 4. 5 5. 3 6. 7 7. 6 8. 8
B. *Students' answers will vary.* Some suggested collocations:
(a) Go through a rough patch, Go through a war
(b) Stocks go through the roof, Housing market went through the roof
(c) Go through with the wedding, Go through with the surgery
(d) Go through my purse, Go through my desk
C.
1. My friend, who was going through a mid-life crisis, bought a new sports car.
2. The government raised interest rates to stop inflation from going through the roof.
3. I need to go through my closet and decide which old clothes I want to donate.
4. What was going through your mind as you watched that film clip?
5. We went through three attorneys on this case before we finally settled it.
6. Nobody wants to go through life alone.
D. *Students' answers will vary*

Unit 12: Get into
A. 1. 2 2. 2 3. 1 4. 3 5. 2

B.

1. There was a report today saying that inspectors will get into North Korea as early as January.
2. He got into the industry with the idea of making movies like "It's a Wonderful Life."
3. An estimated half-billion gallons of oil gets into American waterways every year.
4. You can trace how this story got into the national press.
5. She was really hoping to get into an MBA program.

C. *Students' answers will vary.*

Unit 13: Find out

A.

1. Traveling abroad can be difficult. The Jones family found that out when they visited Iceland.
2. I can't answer it now, but I'll see if I can find out.
3. We found out we ran out of time.
4. It is the job of reporters to find things out.
5. Did you take the time to find out if they had insurance?

B.

2. The phrasal verb *find out* is often followed by a *wh-* word, *how*, or *if*. Possible patterns include: *find out who/what/where/when/ why/whether (or not)/how/if*.
3. *Students' answers will vary.*

C. *Students' answers will vary.* Some suggested collocations are:

(a) Find out the truth (b) Find out what you need to do (c) Find out if she's coming (d) Find out how it works

D. *Students' answers will vary.*

Unit 14: Set up

A.

1. He has already made enough money to set himself up for life.
2. They contacted the creditors and set up a payment plan.
3. Aviana is setting up a low-cost airline called Egg.
4. The state is aiming to set up a job-training program for high school dropouts.
5. I hope he's not setting himself up for failure.

B.

1. The Spacewatch program was set up to monitor the sky for asteroids.
2. The Internet Connection Wizard set up my Internet connection.
3. The city is setting up a telephone hotline.
4. The children set up a stand to sell lemonade.
5. The insurance companies set up mobile offices in Florida.
6. They contact the creditors and set up a payment plan.
7. There is no doubt that he was set up.

C. *Students' answers will vary.*

D. *Students' answers will vary.*

Unit 15: REVIEW

A.

1. Prices are higher than normal.
2. He is acting strangely.
3. Yes, you know how much the car costs.
4. No, they are no longer married.

5. Yes, she was accepted.
6. You scheduled it.
7. Yes, the bill went through.
8. Yes, this means they know who saw the accident.
9. Yes, he goes through all of the flour.
10. Yes, you went through with the plan.

B.
1. After working for a large company for many years, he set himself up as an independent consultant.
2. I knew what was going through her head.
3. The government raised interest rates to stop inflation from going through the roof.
4. The president is setting up a North America Free Trade Association.
5. Route 89 goes through some incredible scenery.
6. The company can expect to come up against tougher environmental regulations.
7. In their early research, the scientists came up empty-handed.

C.
1. Mary went through her father's papers before bringing them to the accountant.
2. You don't want to go through the rest of your life alone.
3. She was hoping to get into the Junior League.
4. The draft has gone through a number of revisions.
5. I don't know how deeply we can get into that.

D.
1. You can use the instrument to <u>find</u> out what your heart rate is.
2. David was going through a tough <u>divorce</u>.
3. The show's ratings went through the <u>roof.</u>
4. I <u>found</u> out how simple it was to get a job in Detroit.
5. The company set <u>up</u> a trust fund in the Cayman Islands.
6. They knew that they would <u>come</u> up against a variety of obstacles.

Unit 16: Come out
A. 1. 2 2. 1 3. 2 4. 3 5. 6 6. 5
B.
1. Ten minutes later he came out of the kitchen with a chicken sandwich.
2. The ex-CEO of the company had to come out of retirement.
3. We were surprised by the sales reports that came out today.
4. "The facts of the case will come out in court," the lawyer said
5. The chairman of the board came out squarely against the plan.
6. The publisher has come out with a series of mini-books.
7. People are expecting the government to come out with some new initiatives next month.
C. *Students' answers will vary.*
D. *Students' answers will vary.*

Unit 17: Figure out
A.
1. It doesn't take a rocket scientist to figure out the solution.
2. I still haven't figured out all the rules.
3. Gazing at the wreckage, he said he was still trying to figure out how it happened.
4. We must figure out how much tax we owe.
5. We owe it to our customers to figure out how we can do a better job.
6. He was trying to figure out how to get us home safely.

B. *Various combinations of the following are possible.*
1. I am sure Sandy can figure out a way to do it.
2. I'm trying to figure why my computer keeps crashing.
3. Some companies have figure out how to avoid paying state taxes.
4. It didn't take me long to figure out that being famous has its drawbacks.
5. Everyone is trying to figure out what the economy will be like next year
C. *Students' answers will vary.*
D. *Students' answers will vary.*

Unit 18: Go into
A. 1. 1 2. 2 3. 4 4. 5 5. 6 6. 3
B.
1. Billions of dollars have gone into research on heart disease.
2. The new satellite system went into service last year.
3. Ken decided to go into business for himself.
4. Since the early eighties billions of dollars have gone into research on heart disease.
5. The report on pensions goes into great detail on the problems facing many people.
C.
1. The son will work in the family business.
2. Her husband is a construction worker.
3. No, people in the nursing field do not get paid a lot of money.
4. She wants to be an actress.
5. Three million dollars has been invested in the Hubble Telescope.
D. *Students' answers will vary.*

Unit 19: Put in
A. 1. 2 2. 1 3. 1 4. 4 5. 3 6. 6 7. 5
B. *Students' answers will vary.*
C.
1. Combine all the ingredients and put them in a casserole dish.
2. Part of the new welfare-to-work program was put in place last year.
3. Every spring she puts in her herbs and flowers.
4. The news from home put him in a difficult situation.
5. He puts in fewer than 100 hours a month at the office.

Unit 20: REVIEW
A.
1. Yes, if story came out, it was publicized.
2. No, if s/he came out against the resolution, s/he disagrees with it.
3. No, they are in the process of understanding what happened.
4. No, she has never been to the desert.
5. Yes, if he's in business with his father, he works with him.
6. A lot of time and effort was spent in the planning stage.
7. Yes, it began last year, so it is in operation now.
8. No, the work that went in was considered valuable.
9. The person was putting in 15 hours a day last month.
10. The frog is in his pocket.
B.
1. The government plans to revise estate laws that were put in place in 1982.
2. We have to figure out what to do with juveniles who commit crimes.

3. When I went into the bank, I saw the long line of customers.
4. He was an actor who wanted to go into politics.
5. Over the weekend I put in a new front door.
6. I went into the National Gallery and saw some paintings by my favorite artist.
7. It is time to put new batteries in the radio.
8. The idea didn't just come out of thin air.

C.
1. The dancer came out of nowhere and became very successful.
2. The new service goes into effect this year/next year, etc. (some future time).
3. I went into the kitchen to get some coffee.
4. It will take us a while to figure out what is going on here.
5. The president came out strongly in support of the action.

D.

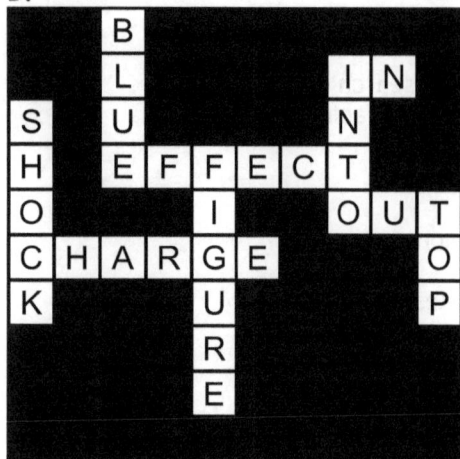

Unit 21: Go out
A.
1. *Go out* is followed by the conjunction *and*.
2. It is followed by a second verb.
3. Summary of pattern: *somebody goes out and does something*
4. *Students' answers will vary.*

B.
2. List of verbs: *thank, maintain, insist, meet.*
3. *Go out of one's way* appears to have a positive connotation.
4. If your *heart goes out to someone*, you feel compassion for him/her.

C.
1. Last Sunday, the minister went out of his way to praise his staff.
2. The president has gone out of his way to maintain good relations with the prime minister.
3. We flirted a lot in high school, but we never really went out together until last year.
4. I pulled myself together and went out to face the cameras.
5. I never go out after dark anymore.
6. I should have been more responsible and read the letter before it went out.

Unit 22: Know about
A.
1.
a. What do high school students know about finance?

b. The more we know about each other, the better.

c. Parents have a right to know about the selection process.

d. He does things nobody knows about.

e. I don't know about you, but I get busier and busier.

B.

1. *nothing, anything, so little, a lot, more*

2. The basic pattern is: *know/don't know X (QUANTITY) about Y*

C. *Students' answers will vary.*

Unit 23: Go ahead

A.

1. *with*

2. *With* is followed by a noun, including *sale, merger, plans, trip,* and *it.*

3. The basic pattern is: *go ahead with X*

B.

1. Bill, why don't you go ahead with what you wanted to say?

2. After months of discussions we finally went ahead with our plans.

3. We have an agreement to go ahead with the sale.

4. The company insisted on going ahead with its plans

5. It is 12:30, so maybe we should go ahead and break for lunch.

Unit 24: Meet with

A. 1. 2 2. 1 3. 2 4. 2 5. 2 6. 2 7. 2 8. 1 9. 2 10. 2

B.

Noun	Collocates with
success	limited
violence	renewed
approval	public
skepticism	major
opposition	vigorous
disbelief	utter
optimism	cautious

D. *Students' answers will vary.*

Unit 25: REVIEW

A.

1. Yes, this means they have a romantic relationship.

2. Yes, if he was aware of the policy, this means he knew about it.

3. No, this means he will not proceed with the plan.

4. Yes, they were sent on April 1st.

5. No, the proposal was not approved.

B.

1. Ann: positive

2. Caleb: negative

3. Michelle: negative

4. Alex: positive

5. Chris: negative

C.

1. We are planning to go ahead with the merger.
2. He knows about the dangers of skydiving.
3. During the recession, many owners of small companies went out of business.
4. They went out for years before he finally proposed marriage.
5. The check went out a week ago.

D.

1. The president has gone out of his way to maintain good relations with the United Nations.
2. Is she still planning to go ahead with her trip?
3. We know so little about earthquakes.
4. Last week the teacher met with three new students.
5. Many parents are going out and buying new laptops for their kids.

Unit 26: Come in

A. 1. enter 2. receive 3. join 4. enter 5. rank

B.

1. The country has come in for intense international criticism.
2. I have students coming in who don't know the basic concepts.
3. Results coming in showed an overwhelming victory for the politician.
4. A management team came in with a new plan.
5. We are waiting for the checks to come in.

C.

1. The US unemployment rate came   in at 6%.
2. The new models are coming in any day now.
3. Your umbrella will come in handy today.
4. The coach is getting me to come in to practice a lot more.
5. Sometimes water comes in through the walls.

D. *Students' answers will vary.*

Unit 27: Put on

A.

1 1. 1 2. 2 3. 2 4. 1 5. 2
2 1. b 2. a 3. d 4. c 5. f 6. e

B.

1. Plans to start the new project will be put on hold until the New Year.
2. The government is putting pressure on the university system to increase enrollments.
3. Italians put about $700 million on their credit cards each year.
4. The school is always putting on plays and concerts.
5. A local law puts limits on rents for poor people.

C. *Suggested answers:*

1. The restaurant was full and so we put our name on the waiting list.
2. He put on weight over the holidays.
3. I put some handouts on the table.
4. She quickly put on her coat and ran out the door.
5. We have made substantial progress by putting these issues on the agenda.

D. *Students' answers will vary.*

Unit 28: Move on

A. 1. 3 2. 1 3. 2 4. 3 5. 6 6. 5

B.

1. The group will be in Los Angeles before going to Honolulu.
2. The man used to work for a small law firm. *Moving on to green fields/pastures* means to make a change in one's life that leads to something better than before.
3. The woman has been promoted twice. Her current position is deputy editor.
4. They are looking for jobs.

C.

1. Seinfeld said no, it's time to move on, do other things.
2. Any comments? If not, we can move on.
3. The officials said they moved on the plan as quickly as they could.
4. She is moving on to her next book signing next week.
5. Reports say Barcelona's other foreign athletes might be moving on.

D. *Students' answers will vary.*

Unit 29: Get back
A.

return to/get back/get back to a place = return
He wanted to get back to the office as soon as possible.
He got back on his bicycle and pedaled home.

have/get something/someone back
The policeman told me I would probably get my bag back, minus the cash.
The football coach got his job back.

return to/get back to/get something back to an abstract place/activity
He will return from vacation and get back to work.
Let's get back to business.

return to a previous state, usually for the better
The tornado caused a lot of damage, but things are now getting back to normal.
It's good to see your career is getting back on track.

B.

1. We sent him numerous letters, but he never got back to us.
2. The important thing is to get the company back to profitability.
3. I will raise that concern with her and make sure she gets back to you.
4. Boeing is trying to get its production lines back to normal.
5. After a series of production problems, the factory is getting back on track.

C.

1. I don't have an answer, so let me get back to you.
2. I asked her to call me when she gets back.
3. He was anxious to get back into the hair care business.
4. He is doing it to get back at them.
5. That gets back to the point Steve brought up.

Unit 30: REVIEW
A.

1. We need to prevent drugs from coming in at the border.
2. I put a couple of handouts on the table.

3. The driver paid for the gas and got back in his truck.
4. The president said we have to move on auto parts and autos.
5. We should put a lot more emphasis on literacy skills.
B. 1. no **2.** yes **3.** yes **4.** no **5.** yes
D.
Across: 3. Put, **4.** Back, **5.** Coming in.
Down: 1. Got back, **2.** Moving on.

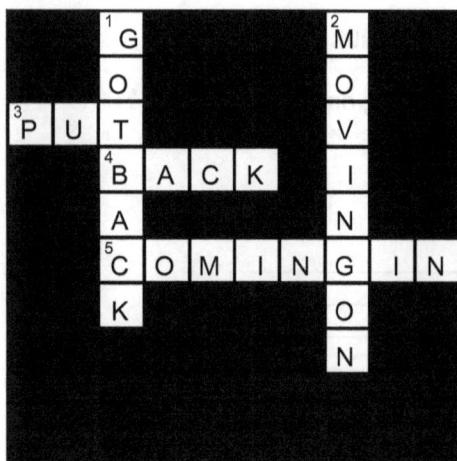

D.
1. In January there wasn't much money coming in.
2. It is difficult to put a dollar value on the merger.
3. We called him several times, but he never got back to us.
4. The finance ministry is trying to get the economy back on track.
5. Put your answers on the board.

Unit 31: Get out
A. 1. 4 **2.** 3 **3.** 1 **4.** 5 **5.** 2
B.
1. There are fears that the epidemic is getting out of control.
2. I had to get my suit out for the wedding.
3. Something must be done about the trash before it gets out of hand.
4. The Fire Department brought in 300-gallon water tanks for stopping grassfires before they got out of control.
5. The board wants to get results out faster.
C. *Students' answers will vary.*
D.
1. If you are *in hot water,* then you have found yourself in a troublesome situation. Therefore, *getting somebody out of hot water* means helping somebody out of a troublesome situation.
2. *Get your head out of the clouds* means stop daydreaming and pay attention to the present situation or be realistic about something.
3. If you *get something out of (doing) something,* you benefit from it.

Unit 32: End up
A.
1. end up+with/in
2. end up+prep.+noun (jail, a surplus of unspent money, a court of law, an unworkable
 solution, the bank account of the senator)
3. *Students' answers will vary.*
B.
1. end up+V-ing (learning, working, paying, costing, losing)
2. *Students' answers will vary*
C.
He ended up needing five stitches to treat a cut on his arm.
He got drunk with some friends and ended up home with no memory of the evening.
He moved to Manhattan and finally ended up working in Los Angeles.
The city government may end up with a surplus of unspent money.
The entire scheme may end up costing as much as $20 billion.

Unit 33: Pick up
A.
1. 2 2. 1 3. 1 4. 2 5. 1
B.
1. The fishing boat picked up the SOS signal.
2. He picked up the tab for the meal.
3. The Bulldogs tried to pick up the game's pace.
4. He picked up some sort of bug in India.
5. The online gambling industry is picking up steam.
6. After a bankruptcy someone has to pick up the pieces.
C.
1. The government may pick up some of the health costs of early retirees.
2. Students need to pick up their room keys between 10 a.m. and 5 p.m.
3. His work includes operating an ambulance service that picks up many of the wounded.
4. Luckily, sales picked up later in the season.
5. Last Friday, a 24-year-old man was picked up at his home and taken into custody.

Unit 34 Give up
A.
1. *give up*+N (hope, drinking, fight, job, hostages, typewriter)
2. One can decide by oneself to give up or refuse to give up, or one can be forced or
 persuaded to give up by someone else.
B. *Suggested answers*
1. He gave up a career in politics to spend more time with his family.
2. He gave up photography to join the army.
3. She gave up a lot of her free time to help new immigrants.
4. Millions of Americans have given up cigarettes.
5. The baby was given up for adoption.
C. *Students' answers will vary*

Unit 35 REVIEW
A.
1. The sun has gone and the wind is picking up.
2. I've given up watching TV during the day.

3. We need to make sure that the information gets out to the students on campus.
4. The businessman picked up the phone and pretended to be working on a big deal.
5. If we are not careful, we may end up in a court of law.
6. We dropped Sam and Pat off at 8 a.m. and picked them up at 4 p.m.
7. Everyone had given him up for dead, but he was found alive and well.
8. It's been too difficult to get the wounded out of Grozny sooner.
B.
1. no 2. yes 3. yes 4. no 5. no 6. yes
C.
1. I've cut down on coffee, but I don't think I can give it up completely.
2. The company decided to get out of the computer business.
3. When I went to pick up the car, I found the car rental company had no record of my reservation.
4. I don't want my son to end up in jail.
5. "We'll never give up," he said.
6. The problems have to be solved before they get out of hand.

Unit 36 Depend on
A.
1. 2 2. 3 3. 1 4. 3 5. 2
B.
1. Depending on the type of hotel, costs range from $50-$250.
2. We've been depending too much on Susan.
3. You can use a hot curry powder or mild, depending on your taste.
4. Residents of the Cayman Islands depend on tourism for their livelihood.
5. What you make of the new information depends on your perspective.
C.
1. What happens next depends entirely on the German government.
2. Many consumers depend on food labels for nutrition information.
3. Italy depends on farming for 3% of its gross domestic product.
4. Mortgage rates vary greatly depending on the product.
5. It depends, really, on what you want.

Unit 37 Point out
A.
1. A noun phrase directly follows *point out*: dried flowers, tree, sites, violation.
2. *Students' answers will vary.*
B.
1. *Point out* is followed by a 'that-clause' (a noun clause which begins with 'that').
2. *Students' answers will vary.*
C. *Students' answers will vary.*

Unit 38 Work out
A.
1. 3 2. 4 3. 2 4. 1
B.
1. work out an agreement
2. work out an arrangement
3. work out for the best
4. work out a proposal

5. work out details
6. work out a compromise

Unit 39 Go with

A.
1. 2 2. 3 3. 1
B.
1. She bought me a purse she thought would go perfectly with my shoes.
2. The safest option is to go with what is popular.
3. People want to leave to escape urban crime and the fear that goes with it.
4. I asked if I could go with them to the shops.
5. His dog went with him everywhere.
C.
1. Once he became convinced of the plan, he went with it 100 percent.
2. You have to do what you think is right; you have to go with your gut feeling.
3. Stripes just don't go with dots.
4. Do we make any personnel changes or go with what we have?
5. We'll go with the company that offers better rates and services.
6. If you don't know your way around, go with someone who does.
D.
Students' answers will vary.

Unit 40 REVIEW

A.
1. Fitzpatrick, went to the United Nations School with him, became a government informant in 1978.
2. Smaller islands that depend on banana exports could be hurt by NAFTA.
3. Frank points/pointed out his tattoos while speaking about his involvement in a gang.
4. The longer hours and new check-in system have allowed more people to work out comfortably in the Rec center.
5. Depending on our initial assumptions, we all come to many different conclusions.
B.
1. a 2. c 3. a 4. b 5. b
C.
1. When they went, I just couldn't go with them.
2. Depending on the radio station, station management and even DJs are paid at some stations.
3. He could look to his allies to form a government or go with a non-partisan figure.
4. I needed time to myself to work out what I wanted to do.
5. He guides visitors through the zoo, pointing out where the animals are housed.
D.
1. They can watch T.V. while they exercise.
2. They will rely on local suppliers.
3. The company chose the agencies because they had long-standing relationships with them.
4. According to this, controversy often goes with wolf populations.
5. The attorney drew attention to the fact that his client had never before been convicted of a crime.

Unit 41 Take on

A.

1. 3 2. 1 3. 2 4. 4

B.

1. The word *liberal* has taken on a negative connotation in American politics.
2. We are so busy that we cannot take on any more work right now.
3. When Stevens took on the project, he didn't know how hard it would be.
4. The latest tax laws take on a new level of complexity.
5. Taking on too much risk is a common problem for investors.

C.

1. You can't ask a school to take on the responsibility for students from other districts.
2. The issue has taken on fresh urgency as fears of an epidemic grow.
3. He has taken on a new lease of life.
4. The traditional institution has taken on a decidedly modern tone.
5. The 21-year-old actress agreed to take on the challenge of playing an older woman.
6. Each of the countries has taken on debt for a different reason
7. The lawyer agreed to take on the immigration case

D.

1. The author was taken on by Knopf, a major American publisher.
2. The animal rights campaigner has taken on some of the biggest US firms.
3. At night, the town takes on a different character.
4. Netscape tried to take on Microsoft with its web-browser.
5. As managers take on more and more responsibilities, they have less time to encourage and inspire their subordinates.

Unit 42 Put out

A.

1. 4 2. 3 3. 1 4. 2

B.

1. d 2. c 3. a 4. b

C.

1. A fire extinguisher was used to put the fire out.
2. The runner injured her leg, putting her out of the Games.
3. We'll put out a formal written statement, and then Jennifer will take questions.
4. The Senator claimed that the White House was putting out misleading information
5. Kickback Records has put out two fine CD Collections.

D.

Students' answers will vary.

Unit 43 Follow up

A.

1. follow up + with
2. follow up + with + a noun phrase (further studies, additional observations, a victory)
3. *Students' answers will vary.*

B.

1. follow up + on
2. follow up + on + a noun phrase or pronoun (any leads, any questions, the official, the kidnapping allegation, them [in this case, refers to suggestions]
3. *Students' answers will vary.*

C.
1. Police said they are following up on 36 tips received from people who were in the area at the time of the robbery.
2. The U.S. Ambassador is following up on the letter President Clinton sent to Yeltsin.
3. In the ninth, he hit Buenos's chin with a left hook but couldn't follow up.
4. The CEO followed up on a promise made last year and raised wages by 5 percent.
5. A consultant can help formulate a new plan and then follow up to make sure progress is made.
D.
Students' answers will vary.

Unit 44 Make up

A.
1. Oil makes up 25% of Venezuela's gross domestic product.
2. We don't know how much money we lost because the numbers were made up.
3. The Senator said she hadn't made up her mind about running for President.
4. Artificial snow can make up for a thin snowfall, but it is very expensive.
5. I had to give a telephone number and so I made one up.
B.
1. I managed to make up the lost ground and finish the race on top.
2. The governors have until Saturday to make up their minds.
3. Boeing told NASA that it could make up for lost time on the space project.
4. The partner made up a story that I was stealing from the firm.
5. I made up an excuse and left the party early.
C.
1.

Women	make up	about 12%	of	the members of congress
Network services	make up	45%	of	the company's revenue
Organic food	makes up	a growing percentage	of	retail food sales
American troops	make up	about half	of	a 1,000-man peace-keeping mission

2.

an executive body	made up	of	representatives...
The committee	is made up	of	doctors and representatives...
the upper house of Parliament	made up	of	representatives...
a committee	made up	of	outside directors...

3.
Group A is summarized by the statement 'NP (is) made up of NP'; group B is summarized by the statement 'NP makes up X [amount] of NP'.
4. *Students' answers will vary.*
D.
Students' answers will vary.

Unit 45 REVIEW

A.
1. The Justice Department put out a statement on the case yesterday.

2. When Stevens took on the project, he didn't know how hard it would be.
3. Women in Iran make up a third of the workforce and half the university population.
4. The police have been following up on the kidnapping allegation.
5. Many companies are reluctant to take on former drug addicts.
6. Some musicals have taken on the characteristics of pop music.
7. The Senator claimed that the White House was putting out misleading information
8. I used to make up songs in my head.
9. We don't know how to deal with this issue yet, but let's put it out (there).
10. It would be like trying to put out fires with gasoline.

B.
1. Who would make up a story like that?
2. The Telegraph is put out by the North American News Company.
3. Livingston strained a muscle, putting him out of action.
4. Several venture capital firms have followed up by investing a further $120 million.
5. We believe the customer should be able to make her mind up.

C.
1. The government needs to help the workers put out of jobs in manufacturing.
2. A consultant can help formulate a new plan and then follow up to make sure progress is made.
3. I felt that I had let my team mates and fans down, but I am going to make it up to them this year.
4. The executive will take on a more powerful role within the company.
5. The inspector failed to follow up on complaints made by workers at the factory.

Unit 46 Get at

A.
1. 2 2. 3 3. 1 4. 4

B.
1. It was sometimes difficult to get at the meaning of the poems.
2. (The) city workers had to take up the pavement to get at the broken water main.
3. What Gail is getting at is really the heart of the matter.
4. I may have to open a section of the wall to get at the cable.

C. *Students' answers may vary.*
1. What are you getting at?
2. I don't see what you're trying to get at.
3. I think I know what you're getting at.

Unit 47 Get on

A.
1. 2 2. 2 3. 1 4. 1 5. 2

B.
1. Sometimes I get on my bicycle and go someplace alone.
2. I think Bill is interested in getting on with his life.
3. Monica got on the plane and flew to California to be with her father.
4. Let's get on with it.
5. We got on the train and the doors closed immediately.

C.
1. e 2. c 3. a 4. d 5. b

D.
Students' answers will vary.

Unit 48 Believe in

A.

1. 3 2. 1 3. 2

B. *Students' answers may vary slightly.*

1. George believes in patience.
2. Everybody believes in something.
3. We believe in freedom of choice.
4. I don't believe in mixing business with pleasure.
5. It is important to believe in your chances.

C.

Students' answers will vary.

Unit 49 Put up

A.

1. 2 2. 1 3. 4 4. 3

B.

1. c
2. d
3. b
4. a

C.

Students' answers will vary.

Unit 50 REVIEW

A.

1. true 2. true 3. false 4. false 5. false

B.

1. Soldiers were put up in inadequate bases or hotels.
2. Academics are always trying to get at ideas.
3. What she does believe in is more power for women.
4. Developers have violated rules in this city in recent years to put up high rises.
5. My mother is always getting on me/getting on my case about my boyfriend.

C.

1. The city's defenders were putting up stiff resistance.
2. Democrats believe in public education.
3. I suppose we were both so busy getting on with our lives.
4. What Gail is getting at is really important.
5. We had to get on with running our companies.

Unit 51 Test your knowledge

A.

1. I'd like to set up a meeting with Janice.
2. The employees put in long hours at the office.
3. I can depend on my brother to help me.
4. What we're trying to get at is the difference between high and low risk patients.
5. I convinced him to get out of the car.
6. Let me go through some of the issues that came up yesterday.

B.

1. I just got back from the gym.

2. He looked at me for a few seconds and didn't say anything.
3. I'm going to be working on this electricity deal.
4. Many of the new products are aimed at children.
5. After I got out of college, I worked in San Francisco.
6. Our anniversary is coming up soon.

C.

1. It's nice to put on a new dress and a new pair of shoes.
2. I'm not going back to school.
3. He decided to take on the challenge.
4. What's going on in the White House?
5. Maybe you should get on the next plane.
6. Let's move on to another question.
7. They couldn't get at the guns because they were locked in a cabinet.
8. The workmen put in new doors and windows.
9. I am hoping to set up my own company.
10. We go through a box of cereal every two days.

INDEX

www.ingramcontent.com/pod-product-compliance
Lightning Source LLC
LaVergne TN
LVHW061226060426
835509LV00012B/1438